Paul

PAUL

Lucas Grollenberg

The Westminster Press
Philadelphia

Translated by John Bowden from the Dutch *Die moeilijke Paulus* ...
second, enlarged edition 1978 published by Ten Have, Baarn

© Uitgeverij Bosch & Keuning N.V. 1977

Translation © John Bowden 1978

PUBLISHED BY THE WESTMINSTER PRESS®
Philadelphia, Pennsylvania

PRINTED IN THE UNITED STATES OF AMERICA

9 8 7 6 5 4 3 2 1

Library of Congress Cataloging in Publication Data

Grollenberg, Lucas Hendricus, 1916–
   Paul.

   Translation of Die moeilijke Paulus.
   1. Paul, Saint, Apostle. 2. Bible. N.T.—Biography. 3. Christian saints—Turkey—Tarsus—Biography.
4. Tarsus, Turkey—Biography. 5. Bible. N.T.
Epistles of Paul—Theology.
BS2506.G7713   225.9′2′4 [B]   78-14372
ISBN 0-664-24234-0

CONTENTS

⟫ 1 ⟪

The Approach

'But without Paul we would never have heard of Jesus!' I said this with some irritation to a group which had been involved in a rather negative discussion about Paul. Paul had complicated simple faith in Jesus, said one of them. It was he, said somebody else, who had literally exalted the prophet of Nazareth to the skies, so that he became a divine being. Now we had to believe that Jesus was the Son of God, and this was really quite a different kind of belief from what Jesus himself meant when he talked about faith. Terribly arrogant, this Paul was; he always began his letters with I. 'I, Paul.' He had always worked harder, and suffered more, and seen more visions than the other apostles. And he was fearfully authoritarian; he was the only one who knew what was what. He was a misogynist, said someone; it is his fault that down the ages women have been second-class citizens in the Christian church. Then yet somebody else added bitterly: Paul made celibacy his ideal. So in Christianity sex came to be regarded as a necessary evil.

Of course the group responsible for these remarks was made up of Christians, Christians who were more or less members of the church. I say 'of course', because Paul is not discussed outside Christian circles. People talk about Jesus, increasingly. He is attracting the attention of Buddhists, Hindus, Moslems, and even modern Marxists. During the profound conversations between Christians and adherents of other religions which are now becoming much more frequent (in a way which is unparalleled in history), the talk is always about Jesus and his God, and seldom if ever about Paul.

There is one exception to this: Jews still talk about Paul.

1

As their interest in, and even love for, the Jew Jesus of Nazareth has grown ('my great brother', wrote Martin Buber), so their dislike of Paul has become more explicit. In their view he was the one who handed Jesus over to non-Jews and presented him to Gentiles as a god who should be worshipped. Paul made an idol of Jesus, and in so doing betrayed his own Jewishness. He became the real founder of a Christianity which denied its Jewish origin and henceforth did not quite know what to do about the Jews. He brought about the divide between the two groups and was also the cause of the horrific treatment which Jews have had to endure down the centuries in the Christian world.

This point was also discussed in the group I have mentioned. We met, determined to get to know Paul better by reading his letters together, one evening every fortnight. We did that for a year. I usually said something about the background of the letters and sometimes tried to describe in my own words what I felt that Paul meant. In this way he came closer to us, as a fellow human being, stripped of the ceremonial garb in which the church had arrayed him. He came closer to us, precisely because he was so strange; he remained clearly a man from another culture, thinking in quite a different way from us. But he also came closer in his utter and passionate devotion to the God in whom Jesus believed, and therefore to all mankind. Time and again it struck us that we were listening to the first man in history who could tell us in his own words what meeting Jesus meant to him, and to all those with whom he was driven to share his experience. We also noted that being occupied with Paul for a whole year did not fail to leave its mark on us.

Hence this attempt of mine to put down what we talked about in a readable book, rather as I did in my book about Jesus. Here is another 'conversational book', but this time about Paul. I have wanted to try my hand at it very much. It has had to be planned in a different way, for all kinds of reasons. First, of course, because Jesus and Paul were so very different people. But they had one thing in common: both of them were a hundred per cent Jewish. Recently an old Jewish musician said to me: 'The special thing about a Jew is that he always has to keep

2

thinking about God.' That's what I mean by a 'hundred per cent Jew': someone who is utterly bent on God, devoted to God, full of him. It is hard for modern people of the Western world to understand this. When we hear the word 'God', many of us think of a superior being a long way away. We feel free to decide whether or not 'it' exists. For Jews the word indicated the most profound reality, on which everything and everyone depends and which they have to take into account; for his part, God is utterly concerned for men, and bound up with them.

Jesus and Paul were both so full of God that they broke through the limits of Jewish belief: for them God was indeed deeply concerned for men, but this meant *all* men. Both Jesus and Paul put their lives wholly at the service of this God. However, they did so in very different ways. And that also makes a big difference to the way in which we describe their life's work.

Suppose we begin with its duration. Jesus' public ministry lasted perhaps three years, but in all probability very much less; barely a year. By contrast there were almost thirty years between Paul's conversion near Damascus, when he began his preaching, and his arrival in Rome as a prisoner.

Then the ground they covered was very different. Jesus' work was done in the northern part of Palestine, which is a very small area anyway. If you were to put a map of Palestine on top of a map of England, so that Capernaum on the Sea of Galilee fitted over Birmingham, then Jerusalem would be round about Bristol. The area round which Jesus travelled was no larger than, say, the county of Nottingham. Paul's work covered enormous territories: the western part of what is now Turkey, and Greece. He travelled ten thousand miles, on foot over Roman roads and by ship over the eastern part of the Mediterranean. It is almost impossible to talk about his work without referring to maps and descriptions of cities.

But the greatest difference lies in the way in which each of them presented the message of their God who was concerned with men. I once called the brief and dynamic ministry of Jesus 'an explosion of humanity'. This metaphor takes account of the fact that Jesus came up against opposition, which is why he caused such an explosion. The world in which he lived was accustomed to a pattern of belief, a way of thinking and acting, which in his view allowed too much inhumanity, too much opposition to what he felt that the God of Israel really wanted. Jesus was so direct and so radical about that will of God that his attitude was bound to lead to his death.

All this can be described clearly and briefly. It is ultimately a matter of human attitudes and relationships which will be plain to anyone. Moreover, Jesus was a poet. He chiefly spoke in images and symbols, and never really discussed anything. When he asked people to have faith, this meant that he wanted them to begin to think and act differently in their lives. To achieve his aim he spoke provocatively, in short powerful sentences, intended to make people think; above all he used short stories, similitudes or parables. Most of them were about situations which were really inconceivable, events which could never happen. A Samaritan (call him an outcast, because he was a sinner, a heretic, or whatever else you like) bends in compassion over a Jew who has been half killed and does everything possible to look after him. That is inconceivable. It cannot happen. It is just as impossible as for a tax-collector (call him a traitor to the Jewish cause, one who has been made unclean through contact with Gentiles, an extortioner, or whatever) to pray and to be accepted by God while a really good Jew prays next to him and fails to gain a hearing. That is inconceivable.

When Jesus talked about 'entering the kingdom of God', as he was so fond of doing, he meant thinking and acting in a different way from the way in which you had thought and acted before. The kingdom of God was like a magnetic field. You let yourself be drawn by the power of which Jesus himself was evidently full. Once he also told the story of a man, evidently a poor peasant, who came across some treasure when he was ploughing. That could happen in Palestine, which had been invaded by so many plundering armies down the centuries. There is no better place to hide gold or jewels than in a hole in the ground. At that time all kinds of stories were in circulation about the fortunate finders of such buried treasure and what they did with it: buying a great house and lots of slaves, making long journeys, marrying a princess. But Jesus simply told how the man put what he had found back in the ground and was so enormously pleased that he sold everything that he had in order to be able to buy the field. Everything that he had gathered together over many years and everything that was dear to him, his house and all his possessions – he gave it all up in his delight at the discovery he had made. It has occurred to me that here Jesus is giving some indication of his own joy, his happiness at being so taken up with his God, to such an extent that he could readily leave everything behind him, his village and his family and all that was there. However, this may be wishful thinking.

In any case, what Jesus taught and what he stood for was clear. He expressed himself like a poet, in word pictures. It has been pointed out that we know more about daily life in rural Galilee through the parables of Jesus than we do from the historians of the time.

Paul was first and foremost a townsman. He was not a poet like Jesus. He had studied theology. He had been trained to reason and argue. And his situation was much less clear-cut than that of Jesus. He had to deal with Jews who had recently become Christians, and he was often involved in discussions with them. The people to whom he wrote his letters often led very different lives, and lived in other parts of the world, and sometimes he had to allude to their circumstances. These are all reasons why it is so much more difficult to give a brief account of the thoughts and work of Paul than it is to talk about Jesus.

My account of Jesus astonished many readers. They had never realized that Jesus was like that. Their picture of Jesus had been shaped by the stories in the four gospels, the most frequently-read parts of the New Testament, and above all by the way in which the gospel portraits have influenced the age-old tradition of the church. In our century, however, biblical scholars have developed what have now become increasingly sophisticated methods for finding a way back to the historical reality of the person who stands at the beginning of the tradition from which the gospels came at a much later stage. For a long time this newly discovered historical picture of Jesus remained so to speak hidden in the studies of biblical scholars. It scarcely found a way into church preaching or even church instruction. That is why so many readers of my book were astonished to make the acquaintance of Jesus as he appeared to the people who were with him.

With Paul things are different. A large part of the New Testament consists of letters which he himself wrote or dictated. So he has always been as it were in full view. There was never the need to discover the historical figure, the real Paul, behind stories about him which were written much later. But it is certainly the case that his person and what he wrote come more to life when people have a clearer picture of the circumstances in which he lived and worked and of his historical background. This is what I shall try to sketch out here.

The facts in my account will be derived chiefly from three sources. First, of course, the letters which Paul himself wrote. Then the book called the Acts of the Apostles, a piece of history writing in which Paul soon becomes the chief figure. Finally the evidence collected by experts who know Graeco-Roman antiquity and Jewish belief in the world of the time, and who are still constantly increasing and deepening our knowledge. In this introductory chapter I shall say something more about the three sources.

While we are thinking about Paul's letters, it is a good thing to remember what a marvellous form of human contact a letter really is. I recently had a letter from one of my best friends who has been working for some time in Central Africa, which confirmed this in a wonderful way. There he was, sitting several thousand miles away, writing just as he would talk to me. He put it all down on a couple of sheets of paper. They went into an envelope. About ten days later I opened it. While my eyes were moving over the lines, it seemed as though he were with me, as though his life was coming to me from the letter: his feelings, his joys, his sorrows, his expectations, his plans — everything that made up his life came across to me, touched me and also had an effect on my life. It was extraordinary to be with someone else as a result of a piece of paper with marks on it. It suddenly occurred to me that in the meantime he could have died, that he might no longer be alive. And yet he was still speaking to me through this letter. . . Any adult will know the peculiar feeling which you can have when you read personal letters from the past. It depends on what the people who wrote them meant to you. I am thinking now of an acquaintance of mine who kept a letter from an old and experienced psychologist. She had had a series of conversations with him, and the letter contained an account of them and a few words of encouragement: my friend was well on the way to having everything straightened out. The psychologist had died some years before, but even now she read his letter regularly. Those few lines still exercised considerable power.

It is good to remember all this when we are concerned with Paul's letters. The people who received a letter from him will have had very much the same experience. One day Paul had come into their lives, and he would never really leave them again. He had tapped new sources of life, had set something in motion among them that would continue to have an effect. He called this a work of God, but he put so much of himself into it that he had really become involved with them. When they read one of his letters it was as though he were there with them, and something of what filled his life streamed into them.

Yet Paul regarded writing letters as a stop-gap. Whenever people love one another they want to be together. Contact by letter is second best. But a letter does have the advantage of permanence. It can be read again and again. And something of what happened on the first reading repeats itself; the other person's life flows over into our own. People could read aloud what Paul wrote or even discuss it with one another. Because they knew him well, he still seemed to be with them, although he could not take part in the conversation, and life had gone on in the meantime. His letters were copied and handed on to others. Some of these people also knew him, or at least had heard of him.

When Paul was put to death, his letters became even more important. They were rather like the testament of a man who had given his life for the cause in which he believed. His letters had been so to speak signed in his own blood. Later, in the course of the second century by our reckoning, something happened which Paul could never have foreseen. His letters, which had always been written or dictated in a hurry, stop-gaps in his contact with his people, were collected together and given a place in the Bible. They were promoted and became Holy Scripture, the 'Word of God'.

If Paul could have foreseen that (but he never could have done, because he expected that the end of the world would come in his lifetime), he would not have written letters. Or more probably, he would have written them, but would always have put clear instructions at the end: 'Read this and burn it.'

We do not know how Paul's letters came to be collected and on what principles those who collected them worked. It is clear that the order of the letters as we now have them in the New Testament is determined by their length: the letter to the Christians in Rome stands at the beginning, because it is the longest, and that to Philemon at the end, because it is the shortest. It is less clear whether the biblical figures of seven and three have had some influence on how many letters were included in the collection. If we were to count the letter to the Hebrews, which tradition at one time attributed to Paul, we would arrive at the figure of fourteen, i.e. twice seven, letters. The letters of other apostles in the New Testament add up to a total of seven. The last book, the Apocalypse, or Revelation, begins with seven letters to seven churches. Seven was the biblical number signifying completeness. 'Seven communities' means 'all Christians'. Now if we disregard the letter to the Hebrews, which looks as if it may have been added to the collection at a later stage, it is striking that Paul's letters are also addressed to seven Christian communities: Rome, Corinth, Galatia, Ephesus, Philippi, Colossae, Thessalonica, and to three individuals: Timothy, Titus and Philemon. The recurrence of these figures is interesting, but whether they played any part in the formation of the collection of letters can only be pure speculation.

All thirteen letters begin with the name Paul. That seems conceited to us. We put our address at the head of the letter and sometimes on the envelope. Then we begin, 'Dear Sir', or 'Darling Mary', and we put our signature at the end. In ancient times people did things differently. The writer began with his own name. After that he put the name of the person to whom the letter was addressed, and then a wish or a greeting. This happened even when a subordinate wrote to his superior, for example an officer of lower rank to a military governor. Thus a letter which plays a part in Paul's life story begins like this: 'Claudius Lysias, to his excellency the governor Felix, greeting.'

However, there is some doubt about whether the thirteen letters which begin with the name of Paul (or, as we would put it, those signed by him) were written or dictated by him. Biblical scholars feel certain that Paul wrote Romans, I Corinthians, II Corinthians, Galatians, Philippians, I Thessalonians and Philemon; they are not so sure about the rest. But it is not as though there is a clear dividing line so that some letters were written by Paul and some were not. Paul had colleagues, people who even travelled with him, and with whom he talked a good deal. Sometimes he also sent them to his communities, in his name, with his authority. Because he had received a 'revelation' from God his authority was quite special, and his fellow workers shared in it. So after Paul's death they too would send letters in his name. Remember that in the kind of cultural world in which they wrote, to 'publish' something under the name of a great predecessor was not unusual, especially in Judaism. The writer of the biblical book Ecclesiastes presented himself as king Solomon. Many laws were promulgated under the name of Moses, and prayers were composed with the name of David above them. In any case, it is important to avoid the word forgery in this connection since that is certainly not the case. Because we shall be concerned only with what Paul did during his life, we shall keep to the seven letters generally accepted as genuine. A complete historical account would at least have to be concerned with Paul's direct influence and would therefore have to deal with the other letters as well.

We cannot, then, draw on all the letters which bear the name of Paul for an account of his life. Nor can we use the book of the

'Acts of the Apostles' just as it stands.

First, a word about Acts itself. We know that it was written as a sequel to the third of the gospels, which in due course acquired the title 'The Gospel according to Luke'. As the same man wrote both these works, for convenience we shall call him Luke here, whether or not he is to be identified with the 'beloved physician'. The title 'Acts of the Apostles' is also a later addition, and it was not a happy choice. The mention of apostles might seem to refer to the twelve men whom Jesus called. But in fact the twelve are mentioned by name only at the beginning of the book. After that we hear only of the 'acts' of Peter, who is sometimes accompanied by John; soon, however, Paul comes to the fore, and it is to his life and work that the greater part of the book is devoted.

The reason why we cannot recount the stories about Paul as history without further ado is that the book of Acts presents 'biblical history writing'. Roughly, this means that biblical historians used the past to give a message of their own present. They related whatever information had come down to them about the past, orally or in writing, in order to illustrate their own belief, their vision of God and man and the world. They thought that this would strengthen the faith of their readers. Sometimes they talk about the past as if it *must* have been in accordance with their own beliefs.

Now one of the key features of biblical faith is that God's guidance was recognized in particular events: this is why stories about miracles and the fulfilment of prophecies sometimes play a great part in it. The four gospels also come under this kind of history writing, each very much in its own way. They usually tell us just as much about the belief and the insight of the writer as they do about Jesus. The two books of the man we call Luke, his Gospel and Acts, are clearly history writing of this biblical kind.

More than any other writer in the New Testament, Luke was familiar with the Jewish Bible. A translation of it was in circulation in the Greek world, and was read by Greek-speaking Jews along with other edifying literature. But at the same time Luke was also familiar with the secular historians of his time. He had clearly had a good literary education.

Now one of the skills that a Hellenistic historian had to have at his finger tips was to be able to reproduce the documents he used in his own style. The reader should not be able to notice when he was reading something that really came from another hand. Luke demonstrated this skill when he wrote his gospel. He incorporated into it much of a gospel by Mark which had been written earlier, but he did this in such a way that the reader would not notice. Fortunately, Luke's 'source' has been preserved for us, so that we can see how he usually dealt with documents. However, we do not have this advantage in the case of Acts. No history of the early church has come down to us other than that of Luke. As a result, we have no possibility of checking on what Luke did in the case of Acts, as we have in the case of his gospel.

There is still a good deal of discussion among scholars about the sources which Luke used and about the real events underlying the stories that he tells.

In the very first scene, Luke gives a clear indication of what he wants to do in the second part of his book: after the risen Lord has instructed his apostles for forty days about the kingdom of God, he bids farewell to them with these words: 'You will receive power from the Holy Spirit which will come upon you, to be my witnesses in Jerusalem, in the whole of Judaea and Samaria, and to the ends of the earth.'

This programme might well form the basis of another title for the book. It was once said that a better title than the Acts of the Apostles would be 'How the gospel came from Jerusalem to Rome', with the sub-title 'From Jesus to Paul'.

Be this as it may, the programme is carried out exactly. Luke describes how ten days later, on the Feast of Pentecost, the fiftieth day after Passover, the Holy Spirit comes upon the disciples. Thousands of Jews in Jerusalem soon join them, despite the opposition of the Jewish authorities. The community of the disciples is one in heart and mind. However, friction develops and seven 'deacons' are chosen, the first of whom, Stephen, is martyred because of his witness. The second of the seven, Philip, proclaims the gospel first in Judaea and then in Samaria. Luke now tells at length how Paul was converted on the way to

Damascus. Immediately after that Peter experiences a kind of conversion which persuades him that Gentiles may be accepted into the Christian community, which up till then had consisted only of Jews. It is important to note that for Luke the leader of the twelve apostles is the first to come to this conclusion.

In the meantime the church spread to Antioch. From there Paul undertook his first great missionary journey in southern Asia Minor. He was accompanied by Barnabas, who had earlier introduced him to the leaders of the church in Jerusalem. When the preachers returned, their mission among the Gentiles was officially recognized in Jerusalem by the apostles. By now we are at chapter 15, half way through the book.

After that, it is entirely about Paul. Luke describes Paul's second missionary journey and then the third, which eventually ends with his arrest in Jerusalem. He makes his last journey as a prisoner by sea to Rome. The book ends with the report that Paul preaches the gospel quite freely, without any hindrance, in the capital of the world. Thus the programme is fulfilled, the witnesses of Jesus have brought the message first to Judaea and Samaria, and finally to the ends of the earth, the biblical way of describing the most distant lands.

Acts is first of all a testimony of faith. Luke believes that the world-wide Christian community of his days was brought into being by God, or in biblical terms, by the Holy Spirit. This belief is often expressed in his writings. Again and again it is God, the Holy Spirit, who takes the initiative, who constantly inspires men to undertake something for the expansion of the church, who as it were sends Paul out on new journeys, determines in which direction he shall go, and so on. Belief in the guidance of the Spirit also shapes the stories about miracles, healings and visions.

Another of Luke's convictions is that God has founded the church on the twelve apostles whom Jesus chose, also 'through the Holy Spirit', as we read in the first sentence of Acts. Immediately after the ascension, the place made vacant by Judas is filled by one chosen from those who, as Luke puts it, 'kept company with us during the time that the Lord Jesus was among us from the baptism of John until the day when he was taken from us'. This is clearly a condition of membership which each of the group of the twelve had to fulfil.

Then Paul comes on the scene. He did not belong to this group, but Luke gives the impression that after his conversion and his brief activity in Damascus he went to Jerusalem to be 'properly instructed by the apostles'. It is clear that Luke feels that an emphasis on the authority of the twelve apostles is important for Christians of his own day.

Yet another concern of Luke's influences his interpretation of particular events, and his choice and treatment of the sources at his disposal. He thinks that it is important to demonstrate that Christianity is not a danger to the state. The Roman authorities came down hard on people and groups whom they suspected of rebellious tendencies, of a revolutionary attempt to destroy law and order. Luke wants to make it clear that Christians do not fall into this category. He does this in his gospel, for example, in the account of Jesus' passion and death when he relates how the Roman governor Pilate said quite plainly three times that he could find no fault in Jesus. He also shows how, although troubles arose in Thessalonica, Corinth and Ephesus after the introduction of the Christian message there, it was the Jews, and not the Christians, who were disturbing the peace.

Luke ends his story by saying that Paul preached the gospel in Rome, unhindered and without any impediment. He goes no further. In this respect he does not give us a complete 'life of Paul'. He must certainly have known that Paul was eventually put to death in Rome under the emperor Nero (58–64), but he does not give any account of that. The important thing was that the gospel had now been preached to the ends of the earth.

Something else is worth noticing. Luke does not indicate in any way that Paul wrote letters, that he maintained contact by correspondence with the communities which he founded. Did Luke know nothing about this? Perhaps at that time Paul's letters were known only in the churches to which they were addressed, and had not yet been brought together in an official collection, circulated among all Christians.

Luke seems to know a Paul who had already become a

legendary figure. Hardly anything can be found in Luke's story of the difficulties and failures, the struggles and the sufferings which Paul describes in his letters. In Luke's story the hero, driven by the Spirit, endowed with divine powers. makes what amounts to a triumphant progress through the world. That is a different picture from the one that Paul himself gives in his letters. Nor is it possible to find very much in Luke's story about the great tensions between Paul and Peter and the Christians in Jerusalem.

Fresh light thrown on the New Testament by biblical scholars makes it impossible for us to combine the events mentioned in the letters with those of Acts. We cannot follow the earlier practice of regarding them all as straightforward history and joining them together in a single story. But this new look at Acts does not mean that there is nothing in the book that we can use. On the contrary, Luke has incorporated a good deal of specific and very trustworthy information. like lists of people and travel notices and other valuable details, which make his book an indispensable source for our knowledge of Paul's life.

The third source from which we can draw facts for an account of Paul is so vast that it amounts to a sea of information. I am now talking about everything we know and can discover about the world in which Paul lived, the Graeco-Roman world of his day and the Jews who were part of it. At that time writers published hundreds of books. Many of them have been preserved down the centuries. One of the reasons for this is that monks copied them again and again and kept them in their libraries. After the Middle Ages, people in Europe thought it important to know about what was then called 'classical antiquity'. Scholars began to study Greek and Latin books again. This cast a good deal of light on the writings of the New Testament, which had come to birth in the same world.

But there were also difficulties. Once the rules of the best kind of classical Greek were better known, by comparison, the way in which the New Testament was written seemed to be almost painful. One gospel was perhaps rather less barbarous than the others, and one letter by an apostle was not as clumsy as the rest, but they were all pretty bad. Devout scholars found this very difficult. Atrocious style in a book which in the end of the day was the word of God? Or should the language of the New Testament be regarded as having a greatness of its own, as being a kind of holy language which the apostles and evangelists used whenever they were discussing matters of belief?

During the course of the last century these questions seemed to be settled. For from the dry sand of Egypt papyrus sheets with writing on them came to light; the first were discovered by chance, and then thousands appeared as the result of systematic searches.

Stems of the papyrus plant, which often grows very tall, had provided the material for the sheets. The pith from the stems was cut into strips and laid crosswise together, then it was flattened. That was how they made ordinary paper in those days. It was very fragile, and could not be used for long in a climate that was at all damp. Parchment was much more durable. This was made from deerskins, prepared according to a method which had been developed two centuries before Christ in the city of Pergamum. Hence the name parchment. But it was far too expensive for ordinary letters in daily life.

The thousands of papyrus sheets which had been preserved in the dry sand of Egypt gave a surprisingly vivid picture of everyday happenings in a Roman province. There were hundreds of letters of the kind that one writes to family and friends, about important matters and about nothing in particular. There were children's writings from school, business letters, contracts, religious texts with prayers and incantations, local government regulations, and so on.

Thus light was shed on daily life in the world in which Paul and the other New Testament writers were at home. One thing soon became clear. The people of the Bible wrote and spoke an everyday language. Alexander the Great had cherished the ideal that the whole world should speak one language, Greek. This was finally achieved. But it proved to be a simplified Greek, not so complicated as classical Greek. It was, rather, a kind of common denominator of various Greek dialects, flexible

15

enough to be a real means of communication for people of very different regions and nationalities.

Of course, Christians as a group had a number of special words and phrases which meant more to them than to outsiders, and which had taken on a new content. They expressed the new belief and pointed to the new way of life which Christianity represented.

I have already mentioned that someone writing a letter in those days began with his own name. Comparisons with contemporary letters also show that it was natural for Paul to follow such an 'address' with a prayer, usually a thanksgiving. Greetings to friends and good wishes at the end are also frequent. I have chosen one short letter from the hundreds that have come down to us, to serve as an illustration. It was written in about AD 200 by a certain Irenaeus. He has gone with one of the corn ships from Egypt to the harbour of Rome and is writing to his brother in Egypt. The strange words Epeiph and Mesore are names of months.

> Irenaeus to Apollinarius his dearest brother many greetings. I pray continually for your health, and I myself am well. I wish you to know that I reached land on the sixth of the month Epeiph and we unloaded our cargo on the eighteenth of the same month. I went up to Rome, on the twenty-fifth of the same month and the place welcomed us as the god willed, and we are daily expecting our discharge, it so being that up till today nobody in the corn fleet has been released. Many salutations to your wife and to Serenus and to all who love you, each by name. Goodbye. Mesore 9.

Since the end of the last century we have also acquired other sources of information about daily life in society, from all over the Roman empire, in addition to the papyrus texts. These include inscriptions on stone, particularly epitaphs, inscriptions on ceramic ware, inscribed potsherds, and so on, some found by chance and some by systematic archaeological excavations.

The results of scholarly discoveries are published as carefully as possible. Then with this material historians can go to work on a particular period or a particular figure from antiquity and increase our knowledge. But in the meantime the finds go on. And the viewpoints of historians do change. People of our time are more interested in the economic and social aspects of Roman society than was the case in former centuries. A letter like that of Irenaeus is one of the thousands of pieces of information which we can study in order to reconstruct the economy of Rome around 200 BC. Because we obtain new information, and viewpoints change, so that we can consider earlier evidence from a new perspective, the study of antiquity is constantly on the move.

The same thing is also true of the study of Paul's letters. Much of the thinking in them can be elucidated through things we know about the time when they were written. To give one example, Paul wrote to the Corinthians that every Christian would do best to remain in the situation in which he was when God called him to believe. Then he said, 'If you were a slave when you were called, do not let that trouble you; but even if you can become free, stay willingly as you are (a slave).'

The last verb translated 'stay' can also mean 'make use of', 'follow the custom of', i.e. follow the custom of accepting the offer of freedom. So Paul may also have meant: but if you can become free, then seize the opportunity.

A young American has devoted a couple of years of his life to a study of precisely what Paul did mean here. He tried to discover all there was to know about the state of slaves at that time: how far their situation was regulated by Roman laws, what legal practice was; what the penalties were for runaway slaves; what prevented a slave from obtaining his freedom; what was the daily life of various kinds of slaves; and so on. He investigated all this in the various parts of the Roman empire at the time of Paul. He then came to the conclusion that there was no possibility of a slave refusing the status of a free man if his master had offered it to him. So Paul meant, if you can become a free man, make something of it in the service of the Lord.

The study also goes into the history of the interpretation of this text: when and why it came about that the first translation, 'stay willingly as you are', was assumed to be the only possible meaning. This interest in how an interpretation arose and became customary can be found more and more in biblical studies. In our day, scholars have become increasingly aware that earlier commentators were also bound by the feelings and thought-patterns of their time, by their own 'culture'. This was even the case with a great interpreter of the Bible like Luther, who looked to Paul for a solution to his own personal problems of conscience. These were rooted in Luther's Western up-bringing, which produced religious feelings and beliefs that Paul would hardly have recognized.

So recently there have been more deliberate attempts to let Paul speak for himself, and hence to see what he could say in his particular situation. We too shall deliberately try to do this, however much we ourselves may also be governed by our situation. For we are no less culture-bound than Luther and all the other earlier interpreters.

The results of 'scholarly' study of the Bible are published in specialist journals. In the Western world there are dozens of them; so many, that no one can keep track of them all. As a result there are also one or two journals devoted to listing the articles published and giving a short summary of them. For the year 1974, in a journal of this kind which comes out in Germany I found details of 117 articles which were written *on Paul and his letters alone.* For the following year there were 130. A similar journal in America lists periodical articles and scholarly books on the Bible. For the year 1975 I counted twenty-four books on Paul and his letters alone!

Fortunately, 'scholarly' knowledge is not everything. There is appreciation, empathy, knowledge which is based on an inner affinity. That is a different kind of knowledge from scientific knowledge. It can be much deeper, even though it may lack the proficiency to express itself in words.

Everyone in fact knows the different forms of knowledge there are, in all areas of life. For example, a geographer can know all about a country, its physical features, its climate, the number of inhabitants, the natural products, the history, the culture and so on. His neighbour may have lived for years in that country and among its people. He knows it in a different way. If the geo-grapher takes his neighbour with him to a meeting of geograph-

18

ers and the neighbour has never been before, he will not be able to join in the discussion. What is said will all be too technical, full of figures and learned names.

In the same way, a Christian can live out his faith in daily contact with that same reality which Paul experienced. He or she may not be able to join in at meetings where there are technical discussions about what Paul meant precisely by this or that, and what his theology was. But he or she, each in his own way, may be familiar with the deepest matters which concerned Paul.

The two kinds of knowledge are not mutually exclusive. On the contrary, each can have an influence on the other. The person who has lived in a foreign country for such a long time may be so taken up with it that he wants also to master some 'technical' details. And his neighbour the geographer may want to go to live in that land of which he knows so much.

So, too, a Christian believer may begin to want to know more about the oldest testimonies to his belief, the letters of Paul, by mastering a number of technical details. By that I mean all kinds of information from Paul's world which can illuminate his person, his work and his writings. I shall try to describe Paul and his world as I did to my group.

One last thing. Not all the members of the group had the same translation of Paul's letters. That did not seem to present any difficulties. On the contrary, sometimes one translation expressed a detail better than another, or the translator had chosen another possibility. So in my account I shall make use of a number of translations.

It makes no sense to complain that you are unable to read Paul in the original Greek. What he wanted to communicate also comes over in a translation to someone who is open to it. I might give as an example a person who is deeply fond of a piece of music which is not played by famous performers or does not exist in a good recording. He can have much more of an ear for music, be much more musical, than someone else who has a season ticket to the Proms and first-class equipment at home. Or I might recall one of my old teachers who kept on reading Dostoevsky, and began to know him through and through over the years, without understanding a word of Russian . . .

— 2 —

From Tarsus to Jerusalem

Paul was born about the beginning of our era in a Jewish family in Tarsus, and as a young man went to Jerusalem.

This is the first piece of information we have about Paul's life. We must now fill in some of the details. On the map on the next page you can see the location of the two cities and the distance between them. I once travelled from Jerusalem to Tarsus in an old Volkswagen. I could tell a number of stories about that, but they are beside the point. Moreover, Paul probably travelled by sea, on a coaster. It is much more important for us to know how a Jewish family came to be in Tarsus and why anyone should leave his family so young to go to Jerusalem.

A Jewish family in Tarsus was nothing extraordinary. On the contrary, there were groups of Jews living in every city of any significance in the Roman empire. Everyone will probably remember the summary in the story of Pentecost. At that time there were Jews in Jerusalem from all parts of the world. The list begins with Parthians, Medes, Elamites and dwellers in Mesopotamia. This area corresponds to the present-day countries of Iraq and Iran. Then follow inhabitants of most of the areas of present-day Turkey. Then people from Egypt and Libya, the island of Crete and finally Arabia, the country to the east of Palestine.

Other writers of the time also mention Syria, present-day Greece and its islands, and the southern Balkans, as areas where Jews lived. The largest groups of Jews were to be found in Antioch, to the north of Palestine, and above all in Alexandria, the Egyptian capital. There 100,000 Jews lived in two of the five districts into which the city was divided.

Cautious estimates arrive at a population of between four and six million Jews spread over the Roman empire. These Jews are often called Diaspora Jews, Diaspora being the Greek word for dispersion. If we add another one and a half to two million Jews who lived in Palestine, Jews must have amounted to about ten per cent of the total population.

How did they come to be so dispersed, and in such large numbers? This is all the more surprising, since their homeland was so small. They came from Judah, part of Palestine, which was not very large itself. The kingdom of Judah was not much bigger in area than the county of Surrey. In 587 BC the Babylonians conquered the kingdom and deported the upper classes to Babylon. When fifty years later the new Persian ruler Cyrus allowed the people of Judah to return to their devastated land, most of them preferred to remain in Babylonia. In the meantime people from Judah, who from now on we shall call Jews, had also settled in Egypt. They lived not only in the fertile delta, but also much further south. Near Aswan, well-known today because of its dam, there was a colony of Jewish mercenary soldiers who lived with their families on an island in the Nile, Elephantine. They were in the service of the Persian princes who at that time ruled the world.

Alexander the Great put an end to Persian domination. When this brilliant conqueror died in 313 BC, he had founded many new cities in the widespread areas which he had conquered. Alexandria in Egypt, by the Mediterranean, was by no means his only achievement; as far as the borders of India he rebuilt cities in the Greek style or had completely new ones built, many of which were also called Alexandria after him. His successors continued with this policy. Of course all the new and rebuilt cities needed populations. They were drawn by preference from distant countries: only in this way could the conquerors bring about the uniform culture which had been Alexander's idea, a kingdom inhabited only by 'world citizens'.

As well as incorporating some of the local population, these cities came to be inhabited by mercenary soldiers, who were able to settle there after their service. On the whole they were

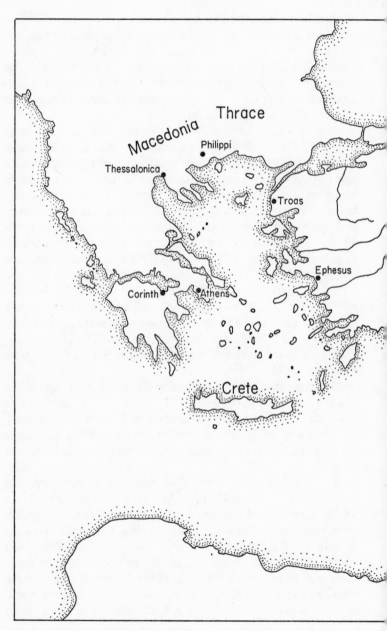

recruited from a wide variety of people. There were also those who were brought to the new cities by force, as prisoners of war, for example, or deportees. At the same time, however, many were attracted by favourable conditions and by the chance of obtaining citizenship immediately.

Now we come to Palestine. After the death of Alexander, two of his successors fought for possession of the land and their struggle continued for generations. Two royal houses were involved, to the south the Ptolemies, who were based in Egypt, and to the north the Seleucids, who ruled over Syria and the wide open spaces beyond from their capital in Antioch. Thus constant wars were waged in Palestine. As a result many Jews left their battle-scarred land and went to look for somewhere more peaceful to live. The closest places were the two capitals, Antioch and Alexandria, which at that time also contained the largest number of Jews.

Although the Jews were dispersed so widely over the world, at the same time they managed to increase in number. There were various reasons for this, and I shall mention two of them. First, there was their wealth of children. Like their ancient ancestors in the Bible, they too regarded a large number of children as God's blessing. Sometimes their attitude contrasted sharply with their Greek-oriented environment. It even seems that in some cities of mainland Greece prosperity and luxury were carried so far that people did not want children: if they did not actually kill their babies, they left them out to die. Jewish families, with their deep-rooted feeling for the unfortunate and the ill-treated, would then adopt such babies.

In addition to this factor there was another one which must occupy us rather more fully, namely, the recruitment of new Jews. Many people in the Graeco-Roman world had an abhorrence of Jews. They usually formed a group apart and did so by choice. Here they went against a feeling which had become particularly prominent since the time of Alexander the Great: everyone had to be alike, 'citizens of the world', and as far as religion was concerned they were to share in what a particular town or area had to offer.

Jews above all felt that this pagan view of religion was

abhorrent, blasphemous and unworthy of human beings. It should be remembered that the whole of public life was permeated with pagan religion. That is why the Jews led a separate existence. They met together in their own houses of prayer, and carefully kept up the customs which set them apart, like circumcision and the sabbath, and abstaining from certain foods, including pork.

In many cities of the empire they were recognized as a separate ethnic group. For example, they could even choose their own government, with its own authority to legislate for their lives. Sometimes, too, special privileges were granted to them over taxation, so that they were able to pay some tax to the Temple in Jerusalem. At the same time, they also had the same rights as other citizens in their city. So it is understandable that their apartness sometimes generated feelings of dislike and even hate.

I could fill a large number of pages with the anti-Jewish comments of writers from the Graeco-Roman world. Derogatory stories about the origin and character of the Jewish people abounded: they were said to come from a group of lepers in Egypt, who worshipped an ass's head, and above all they were lazy: they did nothing for a whole day every week and had invented a divine law to back them up. But what people found most intolerable was their obvious contempt for all those who were not Jews, who in their eyes were corrupt and unclean. They would do anything for one another, it was said, but for outsiders they had only a deep hate.

Yet how was it possible that the Jews who were attacked in this way could get so many sympathizers and even find people who would share their separated fellowship? In our welfare state we can perhaps understand something of what went on in the Roman empire of the time.

The old religions of the various areas had nothing more to offer. Large numbers of people increasingly sought fulfilment more in relaxation, enjoyment and pleasure. But people who lived at a deeper level were still searching. Hence the great success of 'Eastern' religions, philosophies, ways of life, in the last century before Christ. They had something mysterious about them; they came from the East, often brought over by merchants and soldiers.

Followers of these religions sometimes met in groups rather like secret societies. It was necessary to undergo a period of instruction before becoming a member: after that people were initiated and might then take part in the 'mysteries'. Whatever the name of the god or goddess might be, the deity promised eventual salvation, fulfilment, indeed life in perpetual happiness. Even to belong to the group, however, already met the deep need for redemption, for liberation from sin and contamination. It met the need men felt to share their experience with others whom they could get to know better in a community.

The Jewish religion, which also came from 'the East', fulfilled all these deep needs in a unique way. People found in Judaism a steadfast belief in a single God, infinitely exalted above all that exists. He had created the universe. He also had an obvious purpose for it. He had revealed this purpose to the Jews, his people, and it was written in their holy books. According to these books they were the oldest people and their religion had the oldest credentials, a fact which was very important for the men of the time. Through the revelation given specially to them they knew clearly how people could live with the one God, and come to this God. The way of living was laid down in clear principles. Anyone who came to know the Jews and their way of life at close quarters saw something very different from what the slander and mockery might lead one to believe. Then it became possible to admire the steadfast determination with which Jews continued to believe in the one God, living their lives apart from other people, and bravely bearing the unpleasant consequences of this separation.

Anyone could attach himself to the Jews and be a full member of the community. He was then a 'proselyte', the Greek word for someone who has 'come over', joined. A person had to be very strongly motivated to do that. Men had to be circumcised, a painful operation which was not without its dangers; Greeks felt that it was also a mutilation of the body. Gradually so-called 'proselyte baptism' also became part of this acceptance into Judaism. This was submersion in pure water, which cleansed the

26

proselyte from all the pagan stains which had attached themselves to him. Now he had broken with that world for good. He was cut off from the circle of his family and friends and from the whole of his social milieu. From now on he belonged to the people of the one true God and lived in accordance with God's laws.

This step was, of course, a terribly big one to take for anyone who had a position in public life with important social connections. For the whole of public life was coloured by pagan religion. And all kinds of occasions like business meals and parties involved invocations to gods and libations. There are indications that because of this the male proselytes often came from the lower classes. They needed to give much less, and they got much more. Now at last they found a home in the Jewish community. What hostile outsiders testified to, they now began to experience in their own lives; members of the Jewish community would do a lot to help one another: readiness to help, mutual concern and good works were the hallmarks of Judaism. We can also understand that housewives and widows found it much easier and more attractive to enter the Jewish community and to undergo proselyte baptism. Circumcision did not stand in their way, and moreover, as women they had virtually no standing in public life.

I used the word 'recruitment' just now. And indeed some groups of Jews in the empire really did go in for recruiting, out of a concern to give outsiders a share in their own spiritual riches. In the book of the prophet Isaiah the Jewish people were entrusted with the task of being a light for the other nations. They were to hand on to distant people in distant lands God's commandments, the way of life he required. Some Jews felt themselves to be a guide for the blind, a light for those living in darkness, a teacher for those unable to understand, a tutor for those not yet of age, knowing that in God's law they had knowledge of the truth. Here and there Jewish propaganda sometimes became so intense, and caused so much trouble when it was successful, that the authorities had to take steps against it.

People would be influenced not only by this spoken propaganda but also by books in which Jews described their religion, related the history of their people, and explained the real significance of their customs. They knew very well what Gentiles found offensive about Jewish religion and Jewish life. So they wrote a kind of apologetic in their defence, aimed at the needs and the tastes of their educated readers, and removing or explaining whatever might be offensive. This proved a good way of reaching thoughtful outsiders.

Furthermore — and this is very important for our subject — it was possible to share in the riches of Jewish belief without being taken completely into the Jewish community as a proselyte. Anyone who avoided certain 'impurities' could join in Jewish services, read their holy books, observe some sabbath rituals in his own circle and celebrate other attractive Jewish feasts. So around the 'synagogues', the Jewish groups in the cities, there were usually numbers of such sympathizers whom the Jews themselves called 'God-fearers' or 'God-worshippers'. Of course the word God referred to the one God of the Jews.

The millions of Jews spread over the length and breadth of the empire had in common not only their unique faith which determined their daily thoughts and actions, their life according to the Law, but also a link with one particular place in the world, Jerusalem, where the Temple stood, the only visible point of contact between God and his people.

The link with Jerusalem was felt very deeply: every Jew above the age of twenty had to make a financial contribution once a year for the Temple. Where many Jews lived close together, as in Alexandria or in Babylonia, there were special officials who collected the money and kept it in treasuries. Every year the great contributions were sent under armed guard to Jerusalem. Was the city, then, a holy city for Jews as, for example, Rome was for Christians in the late Middle Ages? It seems to me that one could point out a great many similarities. Perhaps even in the matter of doctrinal authority. Where it was a question of interpreting the Law, the leaders in Jerusalem had a definite authority over Jews in the Diaspora. However, the leaders were divided in their opinions and these differences were also reflected among the Jews in the wider world.

It has been reckoned that at the beginning of the first century

Jerusalem had twenty or thirty thousand inhabitants. But at the great feasts, Passover, Pentecost and Tabernacles, tens of thousands of pilgrims came from Palestine and its surrounding areas, and even from further afield in the Diaspora, to swell the numbers. At those times we must picture the relatively small city surrounded by camps of tents.

It is very important for us to realize that Jerusalem was bilingual and indeed more. I have at times compared ancient Jerusalem to the city of Brussels during the German occupation. In Brussels the people spoke French and Flemish and the occupying forces spoke German. This helps us to understand the note in the Fourth Gospel, that the inscription above Jesus' cross was in three languages: in Latin, the language of the Roman occupying power, in Aramaic and in Greek, the two languages of the population of Jerusalem at that time. The people of Brussels, who mostly speak French, could also understand Flemish: Flemish-speaking people living in Brussels could usually understand French in a poster or an announcement. I use this example of Brussels because we know that Jesus spoke Aramaic, though we have what he said only in a Greek translation. Most Christians in Jerusalem who handed on the words of Jesus in Greek would also have known the original Aramaic wording. So we can safely assume that the bilingual character of the oldest Palestinian Christian communities is a guarantee that Jesus' words have been reproduced faithfully.

It is certain that Greek-speaking Jews from the Diaspora came to live in Jerusalem, primarily for religious reasons. It is also certain that they made themselves known to one another by speaking Greek and that by far the majority of them did not take the slightest trouble to learn the local Aramaic. This has been regularly confirmed by discoveries of epitaphs around Jerusalem, which are often written in Greek, with Greek names even for the Jews buried there. Sometimes the epitaphs are bilingual.

The Greek-speaking Jews formed communities, associations, called 'synagogues', usually with links back to the land of their origin. Thus in his story about Stephen, Luke mentions synagogues of people from Cyrene and Alexandria.

Paul's family, which we know to have consisted of Jews who were strict observers of the Law, probably also moved from Tarsus to Jerusalem to settle there on holy ground, close to the Temple. Luke seems to know that Paul was still very young then. For when Paul is arrested in the Temple precinct and allowed to speak to the people he makes him say: 'I am a Jew born in Tarsus in Cilicia, but I was brought up here in this city and educated at the feet of Gamaliel according to the strictest teachings of the ancestral law . . .'

When Paul himself writes about his past he never mentions the famous lawyer Gamaliel. But he does say explicitly that he himself was a Pharisee. Those who know the Jerusalem of those days think that they can say that the Pharisees formed a closed group, characterized by their almost fanatical zeal for the observance of the Law. This closed group was a kind of community of which one has to become a member on the basis of a deliberate choice. Paul, who was fanatical about the Law, must have been about thirty when he came in contact with followers of Jesus, the crucified Galilean. This meeting was to be decisive for him.

— 3 —

Damascus: The Circle Squared

Paul often uses high-sounding phrases of deep significance so that we find ourselves asking 'What can he have meant by that? What kind of an experience lies behind it?' One such phrase is 'I have been crucified with Christ.' He writes this in his letter to the Christians in Galatia.

At that time he was very busy somewhere on the coast of Asia Minor. Something else that he wrote just before this remark about being crucified also sounds very strange: 'I am always being put to death, I am dead.' That was written by someone who was full of vitality. We know that at this point he is talking about what happened near Damascus, about what is usually called his 'conversion'. He felt that it seemed to put an end to his previous life. At the same time it introduced him to a new way of existing, a new life, which he then described as 'being crucified with Christ'.

What happened at Damascus? About sixty years later Luke wrote the well-known account in chapter 9 of Acts. Paul was in pursuit of Christians who had fled from Jerusalem. 'People of the way', Luke calls them. As the notorious persecutor approached the city a light shone out of heaven and struck him to the ground. He heard the voice of Jesus, who addressed him by his Hebrew name, 'Saul, Saul, why do you persecute me?' Jesus then ordered Paul, who had been blinded, to go to the city, where meanwhile a Christian called Ananias had been told in a vision to go to the house to which Paul was to be brought. He laid hands on him and baptized him.

Towards the end of the book of Acts we read the same story twice more. This is very significant. Luke composed his books carefully, and from the way in which he used the Gospel of Mark we can see that he avoids repetitions. He does not like describing the same event twice, so that for example when Mark tells of a feeding of the multitude on two occasions, Luke reduces them to one. When he does repeat something, his purpose is clearly to underline the importance of the narrative. From Acts 13 onwards Luke tells of Paul's great undertakings, his missionary journeys. The third ends in Jerusalem, where Paul is arrested in the Temple. There, at the heart of Judaism, before an exclusively Jewish audience, Luke makes his hero deliver a speech in which he gives a personal account of his conversion near Damascus. By now we are in chapter 22 of Acts. Further on in chapter 26, we hear the story yet again, only now told by Paul to a Gentile audience.

It is a fascinating occupation to compare the three narratives in chapters 9, 22 and 26. Luke tells them in a different way, each one becoming shorter, more vigorous, more with an eye to the main point. The variations also take the audience into account. So in Paul's speech to Greek-speaking Gentiles Luke makes him quote a Greek proverb: 'It is hard for you to kick against the pricks.'

In this way, Luke has encapsulated the whole of Paul's life as an apostle, with all the journeys and travelling and preaching in so many countries, in the Damascus story. In this way he wants to make clear to his readers that it was solely through the power of Jesus, who called him, that the fierce persecutor of the church became an apostle, the witness *par excellence*. He is thus really saying the same thing in narrative form: an earlier life ended and a new life began.

Luke will have heard other Christians telling the story of Paul's conversion which is given in chapter 9, or perhaps he had even read a written version of it. At that time it already had a definite literary form. A number of stories about miraculous conversions went the rounds among the Jews of those days. And what was said in their Bible, the Old Testament, about men who were addressed by God or his angel, naturally played a part in them. They too usually saw a blinding light from heaven. The light dazzled or struck down the person on whom it shone.

When Christians talked to one another about Paul's experience they will have used these familiar images. Luke rewrote it in his own way. It is clear in his version that Paul in the end died a martyr's death in Rome: his call to be a witness (Greek *martus*, which is where our word martyr comes from) to the name of Christ was then fulfilled.

Paul himself refers a number of times in his letters to what happened to him near Damascus. But that is not information that we can use as it stands. First of all, because the letters were written more than twenty years after the event, and Paul could not dissociate himself from all that he had endured and accomplished during these years as a result of his experience. Moreover, when he refers in a letter to this decisive experience, it is not just to present some episode from his past. He is making an important point in the discussion which he is having with his readers at that moment. The basic question is, 'Do you have to be, or become, a Jew in order to gain access to the God of Israel, or has God now opened up a new way to all men in Jesus?' For us today the answer is clear. Of course there is a new way. But to the Jew of Paul's day it was equally clear that there could be no new way. That would be madness, and more! God is always the God of Israel. He has bound himself exclusively to his people for all time. He has given his revelation, his Torah, only to the Jews.

It is difficult for us to think in these terms, but we have to if we are to understand Paul, or Jesus for that matter. For the Jews, the Torah was a kind of mysterious entity. The term refers to the holy book, to the first part of the Jewish Bible, but at the same time it is a text which was there with God before the creation of the world. People sometimes spoke about it as though they were referring to a divine person, a feminine figure with the features of Wisdom as described in Proverbs 8. The Torah was with God before he created the world. When it is related in the book of Genesis that God said, 'Let *us* make men,' to whom was he talking? The rabbis' answer was, to the Torah. People calculated that the world as a whole was simply 1/3200 of the Torah, and it was even said that God studied the Torah every day.

If Judaism had a real dogma, it was that the Torah came

from heaven. 'Anyone who says that the Torah did not come from heaven will have no part in the world to come.' I could quote a great many more sayings of this kind from the first century to show that for a good Jew, God and religion, faith, hope and the future, were unthinkable apart from the Torah. To be occupied with the 'revelation' of God and to live by it was the consolation, the pride and the joy of every believing Jew. Perhaps that should be put in the plural: Jews. For to live by the Torah in this way is best done with others who are concerned to do the same thing, in a community. It is to form a people concerned for God, the real, pure Israel.

There were groups in Palestine who also wanted to live in just that way. We know the group of the Essenes, who devoted their lives to following the Torah, with the highest priestly purity as their ideal, far away from the ordinary unclean world. There was also the group of the Pharisees. These 'separated ones' (which is what the name originally seems to have meant) did not live in the wilderness like the Essenes as an isolated community, but in ordinary society. In that setting they were, however, a clearly recognizable group. Paul joined them. They had a kind of missionary consciousness. They were concerned to win over as many other Jews as possible to live a true life in accordance with the Torah, and to invite others to it by word and example, and if need be by force.

Thus Paul the Pharisee with his innate zeal and fiery temperament came to persecute the followers of Jesus. There is no indication that he knew Jesus personally. That, too, may have been pure coincidence. Around Passover time hundreds of thousands of Jews came to Jerusalem. They included fanatical people from Galilee. Perhaps Paul had heard that the governor had had one of them crucified on the eve of a Passover.

Paul will have had his attention drawn to this Jesus again later when the propaganda about him in Jerusalem met with some success. This Jesus was said to be the awaited Messiah, the definitive representative of the God of Israel, *the* figure of the future. Just imagine that! Someone who had been condemned by the supreme council, the Sanhedrin, and had been crucified under Pontius Pilate! And this madness continued to rage among people who passed lightly over the Torah and put question marks against things which were sacred to any right-minded Jew, like Temple worship.

Perhaps Paul came to hear more about Jesus of Nazareth through his fellow Pharisees. He was a carpenter who had made himself out to be a teacher and prophet, and could also perform cures and cast out devils. He chose to do this on the sabbath. He had also paid no heed to the laws which God had made to ensure purity. Just imagine that! It seemed as though he could not bear proper Jewish piety. He attacked the best Jews, the Pharisees, whose reputation he tried to blacken among the ordinary people of Galilee. But he had also acted and spoken in a defiant way when he came to Jerusalem at the time of the Passover, even in the Temple. Indeed, he was accused of saying that he, the carpenter, would destroy the house of God!

Perhaps Paul also heard what this Jesus was concerned about. According to the man from Nazareth, God would give his kingdom, i.e. his salvation, fellowship with him, to people who stood outside the true Israel. In other words, he would give it to people who transgressed the law, who had obviously been smitten by God, like the lepers, the blind, and of course those who now seemed to be in the hands of the devil. Anyone who reflected on this would soon understand what Jesus was really in process of doing. He was detaching God from the Torah, from the vehicle through which he expressed his own being, the mystery by which he 'revealed' himself to Israel. That is as unthinkable as a squared circle. It is to contrive a piece of idolatry. Anyone who led Israel astray into such idolatry had to be stoned, for the death penalty was prescribed by the Torah, by God himself, for blasphemers and sacrilegious people like Jesus. In fact the supreme council had handed him over to the Roman governor as a disturber of the peace, and the governor had condemned him to the Roman punishment of crucifixion. By being crucified, Jesus incurred the curse which the Torah had pronounced on any executed man who 'hangs on a tree'.

It was incomprehensible how Jews could forget themselves to such an extent that they would see God's Messiah in the man from Nazareth who had been cursed by God, the blasphemer.

How could a Jew be so alienated from his past and from himself? How could he be so foolish?

In Acts, Paul first appears on the stage in the stoning of Stephen. It is possible to infer more from Luke's introduction to the event than Luke actually says. What I mean is that shortly after the death of Jesus there were already converts to Christianity from among the Greek-speaking Jews in Jerusalem. Luke first says that those who were converted were of one heart and one soul, and that they shared their possessions with one another: the ideal Jesus community! But when he begins to talk about Stephen in chapter 6, he describes (clearly on the basis of oral or written information) a quarrel in the young community, which is over domestic matters. The 'Hellenists' are beginning to quarrel with the 'Hebrews' because their widows are being neglected in the daily ministration. These designations can hardly refer to anything but the languages which they spoke, i.e. Greek and Aramaic. In that case, this note of Luke's indicates that Greek-speaking converts had formed one or more groups alongside the converts who used Aramaic to one another (Aramaic is always called 'Hebrew' in the New Testament).

The seven men who are now chosen all bear Greek names, and apart from the last-named, are therefore Diaspora Jews. They are Stephen, Philip, Prochorus, Nicanor, Timon, Parmenas and Nicolaus, 'a proselyte from Antioch'.

It is also worth noting that in any case the first two men in this list were not concerned with practical matters, but in effect began to perform the task of apostles: they began to preach Christ.

The preaching of Stephen, who was 'full of the Holy Spirit', with its criticism of Jewish reverence for the Temple and the Law, was obviously directed towards other Greek-speaking Jews. Luke tells how it finally ended in the stoning of Stephen as a blasphemer. According to Luke, the supreme council, the Sanhedrin, was involved in the execution. We may wonder whether this detail has been borrowed from his sources. In any case, the stoning will have taken place as the Jewish sources describe it. The victim was made to stand on a wall about ten or fifteen feet high, completely naked. The first 'witness' knocked him off it. If the fall did not kill him, then the second 'witness' dropped a stone on his chest. If he still remained alive, the bystanders finished him off with other stones.

This outburst against Stephen made other Greek-speaking Christians leave Jerusalem and go back to their homelands or move elsewhere. There they could not but go on proclaiming their belief in Jesus as Messiah to their fellow Jews.

Damascus was not far from Jewish territory, and had a large Jewish population. The rot was likely to spread there quickly!

It was near this city that Paul was struck by the 'light from heaven'. Perhaps we might try to describe what happened to him in this way: it was made overwhelmingly clear to Paul that the crucified Jesus was alive and had been accepted by God, and that the God of Israel had therefore recognized him as his representative. As Jesus had 'revealed' it to him, the situation was that God wanted to give his kingdom, his salvation, to people who did not deserve it, to unworthy sinners. Through Jesus God wanted to come to men directly, and not through the Torah. This was to square the circle. God now seemed essentially different to Paul. The Torah was at his side before he created the world or . . .? Or was there still something that he had not yet revealed?

If Jesus had been sent by God as his final representative, his Messiah, and if the Torah had condemned him to death, then as a result the Torah had ruled itself out of court.

All this was enacted in Paul himself. In his zeal for God and the Torah he had condemned those who saw Jesus as the Messiah of God. Now in the blinding light he saw Jesus himself as the Messiah. He had wanted to be as perfect a Jew as possible, to live before God, and now it seemed that in fact he was going directly against God.

So Damascus drew a line under his previous life. For that reason we might perhaps say that Paul the Jew died near Damascus. At the same time he became a new creation, a new man, along with all those other unworthy people who had become involved with the Messiah, God's Christ. In his unimaginable love, Jesus had opened up a new way for all men, for those countless people who did not deserve it, including the Gentiles.

How disturbing it was for a Jew to accept that Israel's God had made it known that the non-Jew was as dear to him as his 'own' people! It was inconceivable that before God there was no longer any difference between Jew and Gentile, the elect and the outsider who was rejected.

God had made that known, but not through a report, a communiqué, a voice from heaven: 'This is what I want to happen now.' He had made it known by sending his Son, as a token of love which amounted to nothing less than his total self-surrender. That was really the end.

This cry brings me to a point at which we must call a halt. For Paul, the reality and the crucifixion of Jesus was also in a definite sense an end. For a century or so, many Jews. including the Pharisees, had begun to talk about 'this world', which would give place to the 'world to come'. By the former expression, they meant the world as it was at present, pervaded by evil powers who were at work in and among and around men, powers of death. At a specific moment, which was not far away, God would replace this world with a new one, the world 'to come', which would be completely under his control, and therefore without evil, without disaster, without wickedness and death, with nothing but happiness for the people who lived under the power and rule of God. There was another element to this expectation: the Jews who amidst all the wickedness and misery of this world remained faithful to their God even until death, would also inhabit God's world to come. That meant that God would raise the faithful Jews from the dead, so to speak create them anew, in a form of life in which there would no longer be any death. At the root of this expectation was a deep belief in the righteousness and the faithful love of God; those whom he had chosen would never be abandoned by him, would never be left out in the cold, even in the cold of death. . .

As a Pharisee, Paul shared in this expectation. When it became clear to him that Jesus was alive and had therefore been raised from the dead, it meant that God had now begun on the world to come in this one man Jesus. This was not the collective event which Paul had expected earlier, the resurrection of all the righteous together, but something that had happened only in one man. It might be better to talk of 'God' instead of the impersonal future world. His will, or rather his drive to overcome evil and wickedness and death and to put men in a completely new and perfect situation, had been lived out, so to speak, by God in the one man Jesus. The coming salvation is as it were concentrated in him. He communicates something of this life of his to those who are open to him, believe, and accept baptism. Then they experience something like a transition from death to life, from old to new. That happened to Paul himself in his indescribable experience near Damascus. The Paul for whom the Torah was everything died, and a new Paul began to live, in a new unknown way. He was a new creation. . .

But 'this world' continued, and Paul continued to live in it. However, his life now had a meaning; to involve as many people as possible in this newness, in this faith, in this perspective. That was what God had chosen him for, even before his birth.

This is how Paul himself felt. That was the purpose of his life, to tell Israel that there was something else in God's heart before the Torah, and that was his Son, who had now been 'revealed' to Paul in order that he should proclaim the love of God to the Gentiles. But now I am using Paul's own terms to describe what 'Damascus' meant for him. He used these terms in letters which he wrote more than twenty years later. He was then talking about the way in which the experience had influenced him and continued to work on him over all these years.

— 4 —

Agreement and Conflict with Peter

The chart on the opposite page is rather reminiscent of school. But I have just been mentioning 'all these years' between Paul's experience near Damascus and the letters in which he refers to it, and I wanted to make it clear that there were a great many, and that we know very little about them. Each figure in the left-hand column represents 365 days of intense living, praying, thinking, preaching, discussing, making decisions, among very different kinds of people. That is certain. But it is difficult to say precisely who they were and where they lived.

Our only points of reference are two 'dates' which Paul himself gives in his letter to the Galatians. There he tells of the revelation which God granted to him. He then says that there was a period of three years between this event and his first visit to Jerusalem. 'After fourteen years' he went to Jerusalem for the second time, to a very important meeting. The two indications of time seem precise, but they are not really so. Whenever people of Paul's day used to talk about, say, two years and a few months, they would say, 'I lived there three years.' They counted the part of the third year as a whole year. Moreover, it is not completely clear from what point Paul begins to count the fourteen years: from his conversion, or from his first visit to Jerusalem. The latter seems more probable. In that case we have about sixteen or seventeen years between Damascus and the meeting in Jerusalem. For other reasons, too, we might date this about the year 49.

However, Paul does not tell the Galatians what he was doing during those years. In his account he is concerned with what he was *not* doing, i.e. he was not learning Christianity from other

40

AD	
32	Call near Damascus
33	
34	Short visit to Jerusalem To Syria and Cilicia
35	
36	
37	
38	
39	
40	
41	
42	
43	
44	
45	
46	First journey
47	
48	'Council' in Jerusalem Second journey
49	
50	*I Thessalonians*
51	
52	Third journey
53	*I Corinthians, Philippians, Philemon*
54	
55	*II Corinthians, Galatians, Romans*
56	Arrested in Jerusalem
57	

41

people. Let him speak in his own words.

> You have heard what my manner of life was when I was still
> a practising Jew; how I savagely persecuted the church of
> God, and tried to destroy it; and how in the practice of
> our national religion I was outstripping many of my Jewish
> contemporaries in my boundless devotion to the traditions
> of my ancestors. But then in his good pleasure God, who had
> set me apart from birth and called me through his grace,
> chose to reveal his Son to me and through me in order
> that I might proclaim him among the Gentiles. When
> that happened, without consulting any human being, without
> going up to Jerusalem to those who were apostles before me,
> I went off at once to Arabia, and afterwards returned to
> Damascus.
>
> Three years later I did go up to Jerusalem to get to know
> Cephas. I stayed with him for a fortnight, without seeing
> any other of the apostles, except James the Lord's brother. . .
> Next I went into the regions of Syria and Cilicia. . . Next,
> fourteen years later, I went again to Jerusalem with Barnabas,
> taking Titus with us. I went up because it had been revealed
> by God that I should do so. I laid before them – but at a
> private interview with men of repute – the gospel which I am
> accustomed to preach among the Gentiles, to make sure
> that the race I had run, and was running, should not be run
> in vain.

So Paul went first to Arabia. He mentions this because it was
not Jerusalem. He does not say what he did. To us the name
suggests oil and deserts. Did Paul perhaps retreat into the desert
to prepare himself for his task? People have often thought that.
But it hardly seems probable. The overwhelming experience near
Damascus was not meant to be kept to himself. That the long-
awaited Messiah of the Jews had come and had addressed him
in this way, from beyond death, was a message for everyone.

Moreover, the name Arabia did not suggest deserts to Paul
and his readers. It was the designation of the areas to the south-
east and south of Damascus, which were included in Trans-

jordania. At that time this was a prosperous region with flourishing cities and many Jewish inhabitants. It was there that Paul will have preached his new faith in Jesus the Messiah.

This naturally brought disquiet to the Jewish communities, perhaps to such an extent that he had to return to Damascus, where he was sought by the police. As he later put it in a letter to the Christians in Corinth, describing something of what he had to endure in his apostolic work: 'When I was in Damascus, the governor under King Aretas placed guards at the city gates to arrest me. But I was let down in a basket, through an opening in the wall, and escaped from him.'

Then Paul went to Jerusalem, with the express intention of making the acquaintance of Peter. Peter's Jewish name was Simeon (Simon in Greek), and as the head of the group of Jesus' disciples he had been given the name Cephas, 'rock', which was translated into Greek as 'Peter'.

In his argument with the Galatians, the only thing that Paul thought important was that in the third year after his conver-. sion he went to Jerusalem and that his visit lasted only fourteen days. His purpose was to make the acquaintance of Peter. As the leader of Jesus' twelve closest followers Peter was naturally a key figure. This man could amplify what Paul knew about Jesus. For his part, Peter will have recognized that the persecutor, about whom he had of course heard a great deal, had now been chosen to be a true disciple by the Lord himself.

According to his own words, after this brief visit Paul went to Syria and Cilicia, the area in which Tarsus was situated. But he does not tell what he did there for all those years. He is concerned about his connections with Jerusalem.

The next contact with Peter took place fourteen years later. From the way in which Paul describes it, one has the feeling that it was extremely important for him. This was a command from God himself. And in Jerusalem Paul wanted to be assured fully about his work during all these years, whether he had wasted his energy, whether or not he had been working to no purpose. The real question at issue was this: did one have to become a Jew in order to be a real Christian, to belong to the people of the Messiah?

That was Paul's own account of the years after his conversion. The story told by his later biographer is very different. Luke says nothing about Paul's stay in Arabia. Paul spent some time by himself in Damascus and preached there. Nor was it the men of the Arabian King Aretas who went in search of him, but the Jews of Damascus, who wanted to kill him. He escaped their attacks by being lowered in a basket over the city wall. Then he went to Jerusalem, where as a former persecutor he had difficulty in being accepted by the Christians. Barnabas intervened on his behalf. Luke had mentioned earlier that this Christian was a 'Levite' from Cyprus, and therefore a member of a true Jewish family. Barnabas introduced Paul to the twelve apostles, and after that he was in regular contact with them. His preaching of Jesus to the Hellenists, the Greek-speaking Jews among whom he had formerly belonged, made his stay in Jerusalem dangerous, so he went off to Tarsus.

Here we have an example of what I said earlier about Luke's history writing. He collected all kinds of facts and worked on them in the light of his own views, describing the way in which he thought they must have taken place. In Jerusalem he has Paul supervised by the twelve apostles. His actual words are that Paul 'went in and out' among them. This is the phrase he uses for the association of the twelve with Jesus while he still lived on earth and they were constantly 'going in and out' with him. According to Paul himself, during that short visit he met only Peter and James, who did not belong to the twelve.

After Luke has described at length the 'conversion' of Peter to the acceptance of the Gentiles (twice: first there is the story about the Gentile Cornelius in chapter 10 and then the account given by Peter himself in chapter 11), Antioch emerges as a Jewish centre where many are converted to the Lord. Barnabas is sent there from Jerusalem. He then goes to Tarsus to fetch Paul and they work for a year together in the new Christian community in Antioch. Then Paul travels for the second time to Jerusalem to bring financial contributions from Antioch to the Christian communities there. Luke must have constructed this journey to Jerusalem from facts which he had not fully understood. For we must take Paul at his word. This journey to

Jerusalem never took place.

Having returned from Jerusalem with John Mark, according to Luke, Paul and his two companions undertook the so-called first missionary journey. They went via Cyprus to Asia Minor, where John Mark took his leave of them. Paul and Barnabas travelled inland, where there was another Antioch, as well as the cities of Iconium and Lystra. On their return to the first Antioch they gave an account of their work and especially of the miraculous fact that God had 'now opened the door of faith to the Gentiles'.

We have now reached chapter 15 of the book of Acts, about the middle of the whole work. Here Luke describes at length an important decision which was taken at Jerusalem.

This is obviously the meeting for which Paul went to Jerusalem 'after fourteen years'. According to Luke's account, the occasion for the meeting was a serious dispute among Christians in Antioch. One group there was convinced that a non-Jew could become a complete member of the new community of Christ only if he were circumcised. Paul and Barnabas, who had returned some time before from their successful mission in Asia Minor, disputed this vigorously. It was decided to lay the question at issue before the Jerusalem authorities, 'the apostles and the elders'. Paul and Barnabas went there along with some other brethren. In Jerusalem, too, there seems to have been a group of Christians, former Pharisees, who maintained that circumcision was necessary for membership of the community of Jesus the Messiah.

Peter finally draws the long discussion to a close with a short speech. The reader of the New Testament will notice that Peter's words here sound almost 'Pauline'.

My friends, in the early days, as you yourselves know, God made his choice among you and ordained that from my lips the Gentiles should hear and believe the message of the gospel. And God, who can read men's minds, showed his approval of them by giving the Holy Spirit to them, as he did to us. He made no difference between us and them; for he purified their hearts by faith. Then why do

45

you provoke God by laying on the shoulders of these converts a yoke which neither we nor our fathers were able to bear? No, we believe that it is by the grace of the Lord Jesus that we are saved, and so are they.

Then people listened to the account by Paul and Barnabas of the great miracles of God which they had performed among the heathen. After that, James spoke and confirmed the situation with a biblical text from the book of Amos, in the Greek translation. According to him also, it was wrong to lay unnecessary burdens on converts from the Gentile world. Then he ends like this:

We should write a letter telling them not to eat any food that is unclean because it has been offered to idols; to keep themselves from immorality; not to eat any animal that has been strangled, or any blood.

All this is set down in a letter from the apostles and elders in Jerusalem to the Christians in Antioch who have been recruited from the Gentile world. The letter is then brought to Antioch by Paul and Barnabas and two other delegates from Jerusalem, a certain Judas and Silas.

As has been said, Paul described the meeting in quite a different way. For him it was not so far in the past as it was for his biographer. But above all, the event bit deep into his flesh. When he referred ⁺o it later, in his letter to the Galatians, he was concerned with nothing less than his status as an apostle. This was a matter of life and death for him. Had he worked all this time for nothing? And in that case — but he could not really contemplate the possibility — was the Jesus who had appeared to him not the same Jesus who had given their commission to Peter and the others? The pressure from those who supported circumcision must have weighed on him very heavily. Paul still feels it when he tells the Galatians about the journey to Jerusalem with Barnabas and a Christian from the Gentile world, Titus, who had not been circumcised. 'God had made it known that I had to go' ('It had been revealed by God that I should do so', as the translation I quoted earlier puts it).

In a private meeting with the leaders, I explained to them the gospel message that I preach to the Gentiles. I did not want my work in the past or in the present to go for nothing. My companion Titus, even though he is a Greek, was not forced to be circumcised, although some men, who had pretended to be brothers and joined the group, wanted to circumcise him. These people had slipped in as spies, to find out about the freedom we have through our union with Christ Jesus. They wanted to make slaves of us. We did not give in to them for a minute.

Then he relates how the leading figures in Jerusalem, James, Peter and John (in that order!), did not enjoin anything on him. They extended their hands to Paul and Barnabas as a sign of friendship.

We should go to the Gentiles while they went to the Jews. All they asked was that we should keep their poor in mind, which was the very thing I made it my business to do.

This is the problem: according to Paul *nothing* was enjoined on those who had formerly been Gentiles, but according to Luke *something* was, namely the four precepts. Paul and Barnabas and the two delegates had to take an official letter to the Gentile Christians in Antioch in which, according to Luke, it was said that:

The Holy Spirit and we have agreed not to put any other burden on you besides these necessary rules: eat no food that has been offered to idols; eat no blood; eat no animal that has been strangled; and keep yourselves from immorality.

It is worth noting that the former Gentiles are to refrain from immorality or, as the word has also been translated, fornication. But every Christian has to do that. The translation is in fact an unfortunate one. What is meant is 'incest', in the form of marriages with blood relations. It was by no means unusual in the world of the time for marriages to take place between near relations, even father and daughter, brother and sister. For Jewish sensibilities this was an abomination. So too were the other things: eating meat with blood still in it, blood itself, and meat that had been offered to pagan deities. All these things were prohibited by the Torah (the book of Leviticus), not only to Jews, but also to non-Jews living in their territory or near to them.

But our real difficulty is that these regulations were not promulgated at the meeting which Paul describes. On the other hand, Luke must have certainly got them from a reliable source, which also knew that they emanated from Jerusalem.

It is possible that this happened later, perhaps after the painful event in Antioch. Paul describes it after his account of the meeting. Peter came to Antioch on a visit and ate with Gentile Christians. He ate normally with them, without en-quiring whether what was set before him was 'kosher', i.e. 'passed as clean'. Then something happened about which Paul is most indignant in his account to the Galatians. People came to Antioch 'from James', i.e. from Jerusalem, and then Peter began to be anxious. He started to withdraw and keep aloof from the Gentile Christians, and no longer shared in their table fellowship. Because of Peter's great authority, this meant that other Christians who used to be Jews parted company with their Gentile brothers: even Barnabas (my friend and fellow-fighter, I can hear Paul complain) shared in their hypocrisy.

When I saw that their conduct did not square with the truth of the Gospel, I said to Cephas, before the whole congregation, 'If you, a Jew born and bred, live like a Gentile, and not like a Jew, how can you insist that Gentiles must live like Jews?'

Who were the men 'from James' of whom Peter was evidently so afraid? James was the first of the four 'brothers' of Jesus who are mentioned in the Gospel of Mark: James, Joses, Jude and

Simon. Everyone knew that the Lord had also appeared to him. This James became the leader of the Christian community in Jerusalem, evidently by the time that Paul was negotiating there (James, Cephas and John were at the meeting). It is remarkable that the leadership thus remained 'in the family'! According to an old tradition, James lived strictly in accordance with the Law. That may explain why the Jews who became Christians remained relatively undisturbed in Jerusalem under his leadership in the earliest period. But in the year AD 62 James is said to have been stoned on the orders of the then high priest.

However that may be, the aversion which former Jews felt in their dealings with fellow Christians from the Gentile world must have had considerable effect. Hence the four regulations made by the council in Jerusalem as conditions to be fulfilled by former Gentiles if they were to live together with Jewish Christians.

Paul must often have felt that he was a lone fighter. He himself was evidently so deeply affected at Damascus by the God who was concerned for mankind that he could mingle with 'unclean' Gentiles without any scruples, quite unconcerned about whether things were officially clean or not. Jesus had been just the same in his day. But most of the other Jews who had become Christians seem to have found it difficult to break loose from the deeply engrained pattern.

After the conflict in Antioch, Paul evidently began to work on his own. He parted from Barnabas, with whom he had worked so closely during the first missionary journey. Luke tells us that this happened because they had a quarrel over John Mark, a nephew of Barnabas, who had left them in the lurch during the first journey. Perhaps he was a somewhat timorous young man. Or perhaps there were deeper reasons. Barnabas, the 'Levite', was in theory in full agreement with Paul. But in practice he was perhaps tied too closely to his Jewish past. Paul wanted to go further away, further from Antioch and Jerusalem, deeper into Asia Minor and to Europe, to unvisited territory.

As people of our own culture we might well ask, 'Did his wife go with him?' As we marshal the few facts that we have from the first period of Christianity, we cannot fail to notice that we hear only about men, and therefore only men take the decisions. But James, Peter, John and all the others were married.

And so was Paul. What did his wife think of everything: the meetings, the quarrels, the journeys? Or did she just not concern herself with them because in that culture a wife's view counted for nothing?

It is difficult to doubt that Paul was married. Earlier, we heard him telling the Galatians how far he had advanced in the Jewish religion and with how much zeal he had kept to the traditions. Now for Jews, to marry was a sacred duty. They were to marry, and to have children, for that was God's purpose. The Creator had said, 'Be fruitful and multiply.' That is the first commandment of the Torah. 'The one who begets no children is like one who sheds blood', for the commandment to multiply was repeated after the flood, and immediately after that comes a prohibition against shedding blood. Another Jewish text from the time runs, 'The one who is unmarried mutilates God's image, for it is written: and God made man in his image.' Yet another, 'A man without a wife is not a man, for it is written: man and woman created he them.' Furthermore, 'In the first place among the seven things on which heaven places a curse is the man who has no wife. . .' There is another saying, 'God waits until a man is twenty: but if a man is not married by his twentieth year, then God says, may his spirit vanish.'

If Paul had not married, his opponents would doubtless have reproached him for that, and then the point would have been touched on by Paul in one of his many self-defences. And in that case he could have appealed to his master.

Jesus was not married. He was attacked for that. For his remarkable saying about the three kinds of eunuchs in Matthew 19 can hardly be explained otherwise than as a gentle answer to the contemptuous jibe, 'You are a eunuch.'

Also because of reverence for the divine command to multiply, the Jews had an abhorrence of men who could not father children because they had no testicles. These were of two kinds: those who were born like that and those who had been castrated. Jesus added a third possibility: 'There are eunuchs who emerged like that from their mother's womb; there are men who have been made eunuchs; and there are also eunuchs who have made themselves so for the sake of the kingdom of God.' In other words, a man can be so totally preoccupied with the reality of the God who searches for men to free them and to fulfil them that he leaves no place for anything else, no room for having children. This is how Jesus explained his own unmarried state.

This was one of the points in which he departed from what other Jews regarded as a divine duty, and even today some Jews regard him with suspicion because of this. I recently read a moving article by a Jew about his feelings for Christianity, saying why worship of Jesus as the Messiah was quite unthinkable for Jews. He quoted a Jewish theologian from America who gave three reasons why Jesus could not be a model for Jewish life. 'In the first place, trivial though it may seem, he wasn't married. Most of us discover who we are and determine what we become in the give and take, in the tug and tussle, the war which is a love made marriage.' He then puts the question, 'How can Jesus serve as our model if he never showed us how it was possible to fulfil this greatest yet most normal human challenge? For a religion that places so much importance on family life, this is a crucial question.'

Thus an article by a Jew about Christianity. The same objection certainly cannot be made against Paul. When he writes to the Christians of Corinth about married life (in the first letter, chapter 7), he seems to know about it from the inside. The suggestion has recently been made that his remarks about marriage and divorce reflect something of his own experience. Among other things, he writes there that if one partner in a marriage accepts belief in Christ and the other does not, they should part. God has called us to live at peace with one another. Indeed, he adds, in such a situation how do you know whether you will make your wife behave?

It is a possibility that Paul is talking here from bitter experience. He and Barnabas were to have taken their wives with them on the first missionary journey. But when after their return to Antioch the question of the observance of Jewish customs had been raised in such fundamental terms, and Paul adopted such a radical attitude, his wife left him. She could not follow him in this. Nor could she literally, on his journeys.

It is a possibility, and no more. We have too little clear evidence about Paul's activity in the first fifteen years after his conversion. We cannot fill anything in at all on the chart on p. 41. The question whether or not non-Jewish Christians should be circumcised blew up towards the year 49, after the first missionary journey. Are we to suppose that for all the years previously Paul had found it quite natural that Gentiles should be circumcised on becoming Christians? Or did he perhaps work all this time among 'God-fearers', sympathizers with Judaism who did not want to take the step of becoming fully Jewish? In that case, would they have accepted circumcision as necessary for the new faith, for being a Christian?

The first missionary journey brought Barnabas and Paul to regions in Asia Minor where there were fewer concentrations of Jews than in Syria and Cilicia. Perhaps they then came to feel that for many Gentiles who came to Christian belief circumcision really was a great burden. If at that time, during this journey, they began to accept uncircumcised men into Christian communities ('the door of faith was opened to the Gentiles,' Luke writes), then we could understand why on their return to their base in Antioch there was such vigorous discussion on this point. There were many Jewish Christians who wanted to enforce circumcision strictly, as a necessary condition for entering their community.

In that case Paul will have been led, by the facts, to draw the full consequences of his experience near Damascus, and will have maintained his radical position. Then his break with his Jewish past will have been complete, and that will also have meant the break with his wife. . .

All this is pure hypothesis. Unfortunately we have too little information. It is also a pity that wives were so insignificant in the public life of the time. They could only write private letters, and that was the way things had to be. Had they been otherwise, we might have been able to fill out the history of Paul with 'her story'. . .

— 5 —

The Letter to Thessalonica

Following the route of Paul's journeys in my old Volkswagen, I arrived at Saloniki. This is the ancient Thessalonica — the first syllable has dropped off over the centuries. But I seldom if ever think of my travels when I read or listen to the first letter to the Thessalonians. I am always overcome with a feeling of wonder and surprise.

I then realize that this is the oldest Christian document. Paul wrote the letter twenty years after the execution of Jesus in distant Palestine. So by that time there was already a group of people in the seething port of Thessalonica who looked for the coming of the judge of all men in the person of the crucified Galilean. That faith brought them together in an unprecedented pattern of mutual relationships. And all this came about because Paul had spent a few weeks in their city. A couple of months later, when he had arrived in Corinth via Athens, he wrote this letter to the group in Thessalonica which he had founded.

We have seen that Paul had broken with Barnabas when he began his second great journey. As a companion he chose Silas, one of the two delegates whom the leaders in Jerusalem had sent to Antioch. Silas was a Greek-speaking Jew. As well as his Graecized Jewish name, Silas, he sometimes also used the Latin form, Silvanus. One imagines him as a cosmopolitan figure, like Paul.

The two went into the heart of Asia Minor, via the cities where Paul and Barnabas had founded Christian communities. In Lystra Paul discovered a young man who had the old Greek name Timothy, the son of a pagan father and a Jewish mother, and he became a Christian. From now on this Timothy became a close companion of Paul, who increasingly confided in him.

The three men then went further through Phrygia and the territory of 'Galatia'. Luke seems to have left out places from the itinerary on which he may have based his account. Evidently he wanted to have Paul arriving in 'Europe' as soon as possible. Luke sees the crossing into Europe, Northern Greece, Macedonia, as an extremely important event in the saving work of God. In true biblical fashion he expresses this vividly by telling a story. Having arrived at Troas on the coast, near Homer's ancient Troy, Paul has a vision in the night: a man of Macedonia says to him, 'Come over and help us!'

The first city in Macedonia where Paul and his two companions began to work was Philippi. There they won over a number of men and women to Christ, but they had to leave the small group quickly because of difficulties with the Jews in the city and with the local police. The experiences which Paul shared with the believers there established a deep bond between him and them. We shall see later how this is reflected in his correspondence with these Christians. We need only note here that there were also some well-to-do citizens in the group. These are the ones who were later to give Paul financial support.

From Philippi the three preachers travelled south-eastwards, along the Roman road, the Via Egnatia, which runs from the Adriatic sea through Northern Greece to Byzantium and beyond. After a hundred miles or so they came to the port of Thessalonica. There the same pattern repeated itself.

They found a hearing among some Jewish sympathizers, 'God-fearers'. This offended the Jews and led to all kinds of difficulties with the local authorities. After a short time the three men were forced to leave the city. Paul then went to the small town of Beroea and on by boat to Corinth. His two companions returned to the young community in Thessalonica. When Paul arrived in Corinth, Timothy and Silas came there too, and gave him an account of their experiences. Paul wrote his first letter to the Thessalonians as a reaction to their news. It still throbs with Paul's excitement at founding this new community, which is something else that makes the letter so fascinating.

After the address, in which Paul, Silas and Timothy greet the *ecclesia* of the Thessalonians, Paul begins with an extended thanksgiving. We have seen that an expression of gratitude to God or the gods was usual in letters of the time. A Jew made a good deal more of this and thanksgiving is characteristic of Paul. I sometimes think that those who do not know this feeling of gratitude, the sense of always receiving life as a gift, must find Paul very difficult to understand. Such a feeling seems to be an essential element of faith in one God, the one origin of all that is. That is why Jewish prayer is permeated with thanksgiving and praise. The biblical book of Psalms has many supplications, cries of men in the deepest distress. Yet the name given to the book as a whole is 'songs of praise'. The people who wrote these psalms and collected them together, repeating them down the centuries in their prayers, lived in the assurance that we exist by the grace of our God. We could not exist had he not freed us from slavery, saved us from annihilation. He made us his own people, 'his sons'. He is the God who created the universe, heaven and earth, and he is still at work.

Paul absorbed this way of looking at things with his mother's milk. He had prayed like this since he was a boy, and this was the attitude he had adopted to life. Near Damascus he was overwhelmed by the certainty that the creative, liberating activity of the God of Israel, for which he had given thanks so many times in the words of the psalms, had come to an unexpected climax: in Christ it seemed that God's love was now for all men, 'the Gentiles', and he had made a beginning on his new world, his new creation. Paul now had more reasons for gratitude than any Jew before him.

Moreover, God had chosen him, elected him as his prophet. By means of Paul, God was to bring 'salvation' to all the nations. Paul was able to devote his life to this task. He was allowed, so to speak, to wear himself out in the service of the divine love. That was indeed a favour to be grateful for; to be able to give your whole life to the only cause which was really worth this complete surrender.

Paul 'communicated' by word of mouth, through preaching. But this was not simply the communication of information:

such and such is man's situation before the one true God, before Christ, and so on; at the same time it was an appeal to the hearts of his hearers. Paul was saying this: 'What has always been your deepest longing, what you have sometimes sought in desperation, a meaning for your life, freedom from all its anxieties, uncertainties, frustrations and guilt-feelings, a hankering after really deep relationships based on trust, all this is now offered by the one who is the source of your being, your Creator.'

Paul is sometimes very surprised at what happens whenever people listen to his preaching. They emerge into a completely new life, based on an active faith which is expressed in a completely new relationship with other men who were once strangers and are now seen to be 'brothers' and 'sisters', fellow-creatures who know that they are loved by the same God. At the same time this faith is forward-looking, with an expectation of fulfilment in the near future. Paul sees the response to his preaching as another work of the God in whose name he has spoken.

When the people in Thessalonica formed a new group centred on Jesus, the crucified man who was to come as judge of the world, they were soon attacked by fellow-citizens who were hostile to their views. Opposition was led by believing Jews, who thought the propaganda for Jesus abominable and looked to others to help them knock the new movement on the head. Because of all the disturbances, the Christians also got into trouble with the police.

What surprises Paul is the patience and even the joy with which these new disciples react to all the difficulties. This attitude rubs off on the groups in Philippi and elsewhere.

Paul mentions all this while he is still busy giving thanks to God. When he writes a thanksgiving, he always thinks of his readers, and often tells them what he has in mind for them. Here, he also refers to his first arrival in Thessalonica and the reception he had then. After that he goes back to his thanksgiving. What Paul says next may not seem to put him in a very good light. Rather boastfully, he recalls that his dealings with the people of Thessalonica have been beyond reproach.

At this point we have to draw on our third source, the mass of information which is not contained in the letter, but which will have been familiar to Paul and his readers. In Thessalonica, too, there was a lively market in religion. Just about everything was offered because the demand was so varied. As a parallel we might think of all the ways in which sex is exploited in our society. At that time, however, what countless confused and uprooted people looked for was some form of religion. They could enrol in secret societies in order to take part in 'mysteries'. Here, they might find redemption by being sprinkled with the blood of a deity and thus sharing in his or her new life. Philosophers recruited followers of their teaching, which claimed to solve life's riddles. It was possible to enrol in courses in Eastern techniques aimed at achieving a spiritual state. Miracle-workers praised their own healing powers and soothsayers offered a chance to face the future with a quiet mind. But it all cost money. There was a good deal of haggling. The propagandists did all they could to win clients, and each tried to outbid the other.

Paul asks the recently converted Thessalonians to remember how he and his companions stood out from the vendors of religious wares as a race apart. They did not ask for any money. They tried to support themselves. They had spent all the time at their disposal talking with those who were interested and praying with those who had become believers. Paul evidently had the gift of taking a personal interest in everyone, and concerning himself closely with a few, without seeming to be overbearing. In this passage he compares himself to a mother who cares for her family, and to a father who admonishes and encourages his older children.

Paul places strong emphasis on manual work. He did not want to take any money at all from the people to whom he had preached the faith. His reason for this is clear. How can anyone claim to be the messenger of a God who has loved to the uttermost, who has really given his all, if he profits from what he has to say? Paul did not want to seem in any way like the vendors of religions, the merchants of 'salvation'. Only through utter unselfishness on his part could his words appear as the words of the God who had shown the meaning of self-surrender; only in this way could they be effective for those to whom they were addressed.

This, then, is the way in which Paul worked in Thessalonica. While remembering his stay with gratitude, in the same breath he also seems to be attacking the Jews. You Thessalonians, he says, have a good deal to put up with from your fellow-country-men, just as the Jewish Christians at home in Judaea have a great deal to put up with from the Jews there, 'who killed both the Lord Jesus and the prophets, and drove us out, and displease God and oppose all men by hindering us from speaking to the Gentiles that they may be saved — so as always to fill up the measure of their sins. But God's wrath has come upon them at last.'

It is well to remember here that the theme of murdering the prophets had developed within Judaism itself. It can be found some centuries before Christ in the penitential prayer in Nehemiah 9. Among the crimes which Israel itself acknowledged was the killing of the prophets whom God had sent to his people. This was a common theme in public confessions of sin. Jesus' lament over Jerusalem, the city which 'kills the prophets and stones those who are sent to her', repeats the old refrain.

The members of the Sanhedrin also knew it from their penitential prayers. But it never entered their heads that Jesus might be a prophet. They identified God far too closely with the Torah. For Christians, however, Jesus was a prophet and more. That is why they took up the theme of the Bible again, as Paul does here. The vigorous opposition of Jews to Christianity and the recruitment of Christians from among the Gentiles follows the same line.

After this attack Paul talks about his longing to see the Thessalonians again. He describes what it feels like to be separated from them, and how he hopes to visit them again soon. It is a point of honour for him that the community should stand up under pressure and grow more mature. Indeed, it is more than a point of honour: that is why he has been called by God, his *raison d'être*. When the Lord comes to give judgment, which will be soon, Paul will stand or fall by the condition of the communi-

58

ties which he has founded. Since he cannot visit them in person, he has to resort to a letter.

After all these personal details, incorporated in expressions of gratitude, Paul expands on three points. First of all he underlines the need for sexual purity. Anyone who has come to know the true God with his emotions, and not just in theory, finding the purpose of life in him, is bound to respect fellow human beings. In that case the most intimate relationship between a man and a woman should certainly be seen as something sacred. To come between them as a third party, as an intruder, is not only to wrong others but also to misunderstand the very nature of God.

With this warning Paul moves on to the second point: he speaks of the love which believers must have, first of all for one another, then for other Christians in their area, and finally even for their Gentile fellow-citizens, who are outsiders. In their enthusiasm, and above all in their expectation of the speedy reappearance of Christ, the new converts might be inclined to stop working with an eye to the future, to live from hand to mouth, and ultimately rely on others for their needs.

Paul's third point is probably the most difficult. This completely new way of belonging together meant that people could be intensely happy and try to live a better life, but there was one power against which they could do nothing. That was death, the irresistible power which puts an end to everything. Death destroys fellowship, and separates men from one another, sometimes very suddenly, sometimes very cruelly, and always irrevocably.

After Paul's departure, one or two members of the new community had died. Like all the rest, they had looked forward with elation to the coming of Jesus, his glorious appearance as judge and lord. Now they were dead, so they would not be there. That raised all kinds of questions. Had they done something wrong which made them lose their privileges?

Paul now writes to the community to assure them that they need not worry about those who have died:

We who are alive, who are left until the coming of the

Lord, shall not precede those who have fallen asleep. For the Lord himself will descend from heaven with a cry of command, with the archangel's call, and with the sound of the trumpet of God. And the dead in Christ will rise first; then we who are alive, who are left, shall be caught up together with them in the clouds to meet the Lord in the air; and so we shall always be with the Lord.

The bereaved are to comfort one another with this assurance. That is the first thing. But secondly, it is also certain that we do not know and cannot know the date of the coming of Jesus. So we must always be prepared for it. That means that we are not to go through life as though we were asleep, stupefied by a life of pleasure or dully acquiescent. We are always to be fresh and awake, with a keen eye for the things that really matter in life. Only in this way can we be true to our calling, which according to Paul is that Christ has died for us, so that whether we wake or sleep we might live with him. So keeping a constant watch for him, we must comfort and support one another.

According to what we know of Paul from his letter, he never doubted that God would soon put an end to history, to 'this world'. Then Jesus the crucified one would appear as the judge of all men. It would happen very soon, for Paul expected that he would live to see it. And even if he were by chance to die earlier, or to be put to death, at all events his generation would share in the end. But it never came to that, at least as Paul imagined it. Still, where did he get this idea from, and what can it mean for us?

Just now, when I was discussing Paul's conversion, I referred to the Jewish expectation that God would replace 'this world' with a new world which was truly good. If I were writing more formally, I might put it like this: there are two aspects to this expectation with which it is very difficult for us to sympathize. We cannot accept either the belief from which the expectation arose or the primitive view of the world which made it possible.

We shall begin with the belief. Ancient Israel often saw its God Yahweh in the form of an ideal ancient near-eastern king. He wanted nothing but the complete happiness of his subjects, so he stood for law and justice; he was on the side of the oppressed and the poor, the widows and the orphans. Some prophets put it in pictorial form: one day Yahweh would rule from his temple in Jerusalem over all people; on Zion, the holy mountain, they would learn to live in peace with one another, and then they would beat their swords into ploughshares . . .

When these visions included a human king from the line of David, such a ruler was seen as God's representative. He would therefore put an end to all injustice, root out all evildoers, establish justice among men and nations, and thus bring about an ideal society.

In the last centuries before Christ the visions became increasingly unrealistic. The really great decisions were made a long way from Palestine, by the Medes and Persians, the Greeks, and finally the Romans. It was no use supposing that Jerusalem, that city in the desolate hill-country of Judaea, without any political significance, would ever be the centre of the world. In the meantime the godless nations pressed on with their wars and their empires. In the second century before Christ, a Greek king committed the most appalling crime that a Jew could think of: he placed an idol in the temple of Israel's God. God could only react to this by making an end of the whole corrupt world, and it would not be long before he did just that. But he would certainly never give up his real purpose, which was to create a world of men who would recognize him as their God and Lord, and so would live happily together. That meant making a new world.

The more intolerable the situation in Palestine under the Romans became, the more eagerly the Jews looked forward to God's final intervention. In the time of Jesus a whole literature was produced about it. The writers gave free rein to their fantasy. They tried to depict how it would all happen, the end of this evil world and the beginning of the world to come. This was the sort of literature for oppressed people, a kind of liberation poetry.

The writers borrowed a good deal from one another. So the stage picture of the last great day was crowded out with scenery: there were earthquakes and fire and natural disasters, angels and archangels, trumpets and clouds. Often, too, there was a divine representative, like the Davidic king in the earlier visions. This time, however, he was depicted as a heavenly figure, an almost godlike being, 'in the form of a Son of man'.

Some writers also described what would happen shortly before all this: there would be 'signs' by which one could tell that the dawning of the kingdom of God was imminent. They even calculated how many units of time had to elapse before the end.

There is no need to make a long digression about John the Baptist and Jesus at this point. We know that both of them were preoccupied with what would happen in a short time. But they did not get caught up in descriptions and calculations; they summoned the Jews to repentance. What was special about Jesus was his incredible claim: God was already on his way in what Jesus said and did. The new world was beginning now. At the same time, though, Jesus believed that its real and definitive form was still to come. That was God's work alone, and no human being could influence it. God would act very quickly, within the life-span of Jesus' generation.

Because of all this, Jesus' disciples were much more expectant after Passover than the other Jews. They had the positive assurance of Jesus that God's kingdom was now imminent, and this was still fixed in their memory. Jesus had now been caught up to be with God, but he would be the central figure in the judgment to come: he would be the Son of man from heaven. It was difficult to talk about his return without using the traditional imagery and stage properties. Paul himself has to do this in his letter to the Thessalonians.

When the Jewish Christians met together, right from the very beginning, one might often hear the cry 'Maranatha!'. This can mean 'Our Lord has come', and also 'Come, Lord'. The second meaning will certainly be the right one here. This Aramaic exclamation was so meaningful that the Greek-speaking Christians took it over without translating it.

To describe the imminent appearance of Christ, Paul uses a term which was already in vogue among other Greek-speaking Christians: 'parousia'. In the Greek world this meant 'presence', 'coming'. It was used whenever a great ruler came on a visit to one of his cities. At that time there would be great festivities and games; people would form a procession to meet the ruler, to welcome him and to accompany him into the city. Criminals in prison there would tremble at the thought of the judgment that he would pronounce over them at the parousia. So among Christians the word became a kind of technical term for the consummation that they knew to be near.

This Jewish-Christian expectation of the coming end of this evil world was derived from belief in the one God who cares for his people. He will never be untrue to his nature, so it is certain that the new world he is to make will be good. In this world there would be no more injustice, no more tears and no more death; everyone would be completely fulfilled and infinitely happy. The Jewish Christians described God's care for his people in quite specific terms, and they could do that because their view of the world was so different from ours. I think it very important that we should understand this clearly.

According to the Jewish Bible, God had made the world only four thousand years previously. He created Adam on the sixth day. The Bible mentions a son of Adam called Seth, and then Seth's son, and then Seth's son's son, and so the line goes on, from one man to another, all of whom are given names, until we come to Abraham. After Abraham the pattern continues in essentially the same way down to the present. Pious Jews in the time of Jesus all had family trees which went back to someone in the Bible. Paul once wrote that he came from the tribe of Benjamin, and his family doubtless had a genealogy to prove the fact. There is another remarkable thing: whenever we are given the name of a rabbi of the time, we are almost always told his father's name. The fact that Paul nowhere gives the name of *his* father may be connected with his experience of as it were being born again. The past was a different existence altogether.

During this compact history of less than four thousand years, God had constantly cared for his people. One needed only to think of his conversation with Cain, of Noah and the flood, of Abraham and the twelve ancestors of Israel, of Moses and the exodus, David and the great prophets . . .

God had constantly intervened and given a new twist to history. Because of this it was easy to imagine that he would soon intervene again, in a definitive way. He would purge this earth of all wickedness and all evil once and for all, and then he would restore to human existence the splendour that he had intended for all mankind, his 'image and likeness'.

We may well call such a vision and such an expectation 'primitive'. For us, human history does not have so short a duration; it is not so compact and not so directly guided by God. Even as schoolchildren, we became familiar with enormous spans of time while learning about the first men who were descended from the apes: they lived hundreds of thousands of years ago, in an incredibly remote past. We were also taught about the planets, the stars and the Milky Way, and we learned to use the words 'light year' — the distance that light covers in the course of a year. It is an unimaginable distance, and now we read that signals have been received from space which were transmitted four thousand million light years ago . . .

We never talk about the God who is at work in that immeasurable universe and in our world. We talk about the 'processes' which take place in it, so to speak, from within.

So what are we to make of the expectations of Paul and his fellow Christians? For them everything seemed so near, from the time of the first men onwards, and God was constantly involved with the events of history. For us, on the other hand, these things are all in the immeasurable past, and a God who 'intervenes' in the same way as the God of the Bible has become inconceivable.

I think it would be a good thing to leave the question 'What should we make of it?' on one side, while we listen to Paul for a bit longer. The way in which someone whom we know pictures the future need not be important in itself. At best, we may be interested enough to listen. But we see it in a different light when we realize that the person is really trying to describe his present beliefs and endeavours, his hopes and his longings, all of which affect the way in which he deals with his fellow men.

— 6 —

Opportunities in Corinth

Paul always wanted to do more than he could. He felt that he had had to leave Thessalonica much too early, and his letter to the Thessalonians shows that he wanted to go back there quickly. At the same time he had Corinth in his programme. Work there would certainly occupy all his energies. For Corinth was the largest city in Greece, a unique meeting-point in the Graeco-Roman world; it was the most 'modern' city of the time, with nothing but new buildings.

In 146 BC the Roman general Mummius had totally destroyed the old Corinth, 'eradicated' it. It was an age-old practice of victors and founders of empires to destroy cities they had conquered, and with their soldiers and slaves they made a more thorough job of it than we do with our bombs. About a century later, towards 44 BC, Julius Caesar gave orders for it to be rebuilt. Corinth was to become a Roman 'colony'. Not long after that, the emperor Augustus made it the capital of the new Roman 'province' of Achaea, which covered central Greece and the great peninsula of the Peloponnese.

From the map on pp. 22-23, you can see why the rebuilt Corinth came to flourish so quickly as a trading city. It lay on a kind of dam between the Aegean Sea to the east, and the Adriatic. The two parts of the Roman Empire met here: Asia Minor and what lay beyond: and to the west, Italy and more distant lands. Merchandise was transported over the narrow strip of land between the western harbour of Lechaion and the eastern harbour of Cenchreae. Under the emperor Nero, one of many attempts was made to dig a canal, but even Roman engineers had to give up the plan.

In addition to handling foreign goods and Greek products and dealing in currency (it was a great banking centre), Corinth also had its own industries, including metal working and pottery. Greek, Roman and Eastern deities were worshipped in the numerous temples. Another sign of the prosperity of the new Corinth was its sponsorship of the old Isthmian Games, which the city financed from its own funds. These games competed with the famous Olympic Games, which were held in honour of Zeus every four years in Olympia on the other side of the Peloponnese. The Isthmian Games were held every two years, in the spring, in honour of Poseidon, and included chariot races, athletics and music. At that time, not only sportsmen and musicians, but also tens of thousands of visitors came to Corinth.

The large population there was a mixed bunch. Some of them originally came from Italy: they were veterans and freed slaves who had been settled there as inhabitants of the new 'colony'. This gave the city a marked Roman character. But many of its inhabitants were, of course, Greek and some were from further afield. And of course many Jews also came to live there.

What we know about Corinth derives largely from writings of the time, and also from archaeological discoveries. The inner city of Corinth has been systematically excavated. The foundations of all kinds of buildings were uncovered in the centre. They formed a central square with shops round the sides, called the meat market. There were also colonnades, covered halls for great meetings (basilica was the Roman term for them), baths, government buildings, and above all temples. Before the coming of the Romans there was a temple to the goddess Artemis on the huge rock near the city, which employed a thousand girls as prostitutes for the pious worshippers of the goddess. This form of worship, which seems remarkable to us, was by no means exceptional in antiquity. And it was certainly very much a pagan preoccupation when Paul came to Corinth.

A couple of years later he wrote to the Christians there that he had been anxious and even nervous on his first arrival at the city. That is understandable. To walk on your own into such a teeming city, first through the suburbs with their stately houses and hovels standing side by side, and then amidst the hubbub of the centre, with your heart full of a message about a crucified man which was vitally important for everyone, was quite an enterprise.

Paul arrived in Corinth after a short visit to Athens. Had his mood anything to do with his experiences in that city? Compared to the new buildings and bustling life of Corinth, Athens was really a half-dead city, its glory faded. Politically and economically it had virtually no significance. It attracted tourists because of its splendid buildings, reminiscent of its great past. It was really a kind of museum. And it was still a university city, with philosophy as the main subject. Various schools of thought were represented, going back to the great teachers of earlier days. Each group discussed in its own way the great questions which presented themselves to any thinking man: Where does everything come from, and why does it exist? How are we to imagine the beginning of everything? How can a purely spiritual creator have contact with the material world of which man is a part, unless man also has a spiritual element in him, something like a soul? What should a man expect after death? What is the sense of leading a good life? What is the good? What restrains one from making an end to life if happiness is no longer possible? What is life, anyway? What is one's fellow man worth? Is a slave a fellow man? And so on. If you were interested in speculative conversations, then Athens was the place for you.

Is that why Paul went there? Or had the boat in which he was sailing to Corinth stopped at Athens for a day or so? Anyone who travelled in Greece had to have seen Athens. It was a 'must'. We do not know Paul's reasons for going. Be that as it may, in Acts 17 Luke has made a masterly story out of his visit. In a couple of lines he conjures up how a believing Jew felt in such a pagan city, and also shows how the snobbish, yet curious, Athenians reacted to Paul. They brought him to the Areopagus. That was originally the name of a hill in the centre, close to the Acropolis, the 'hill of the God Ares'. In earlier days the court of justice was situated there. At that time Areopagus was the name of the college of judges, and remained so, even when the college was housed elsewhere. It seems that in the Roman period this college still had authority in affairs of religion and education. Luke may want to set his hero's speech away from the bustle of the city on the quiet hill, making it a kind of open lecture, or he may have in mind a defence before an official committee, the Areopagus. Whichever is the case, he has worked out Paul's message with great care.

Its starting point is not a saying from the Bible, which was an unfamiliar book to Gentiles, but something that Paul had observed. He had seen an altar which was dedicated 'to an unknown God'. He, Paul, had now come to make known the true God to the Athenians. This God was the creator of all things, who did not live in a temple, and did not need men's sacrifices. After these three statements about God, Paul also says three things about men: the one God brought them all forth from one ancestor; he made the earth and the world of nature for the welfare of all men; and his purpose in so doing was that men should seek for him and find him. With a couple of well-known quotations from Greek poets, Paul then points to the affinity between man and the one God; this is not recognized by those who make idols. However, Paul concludes, God does not take it amiss that men should act in this way, but now 'he commands all men everywhere to repent, because he has fixed a day on which he will judge the world in righteousness by a man whom he has appointed, and of this he has given assurance to all men by raising him from the dead . . .'

At this reference to the resurrection of a dead man and the implication that the dead have new bodies, the Athenians give up. For them this is a nonsensical idea. Their view was that a man should try to escape the limitations of his bodily existence and that in the end only the spiritual part of him remained. Some hearers mocked Paul for his speech, but others went off saying, 'We will talk to you about this on another occasion.'

Luke names two people who accepted Paul's message, but no community of Christians was formed in fusty Athens. There was far more chance of this in Corinth, a city which was not weighed down by the past, and where men were much more receptive to new ideas. Certainly the more thoughtful people. those who were more or less intellectual, were on the lookout for a view of life, a way of thinking and behaving which had more to offer than their everyday existence. So this was a promising area for Paul. But where was he to begin in such a city?

Paul may well have begun by asking where Jews lived. Or did he first nose around in the streets where trades were carried on? He himself had a trade: 'tentmaker', the Greek word is sometimes translated, but 'leather-worker' might be a better rendering. Anyway, he had to see how he was going to earn his living.

Luke says that he found work, and also accommodation, in the household of a Jew with the Latin name Aquila, 'eagle'. His wife was called Priscilla, a diminutive form of the name Prisca. This Jewish couple had once lived in Rome, but under the emperor Claudius all Jews had been forced to leave Rome. So Luke tells us, and his information has been confirmed by a historian of the time called Suetonius, in his life of the emperor Claudius. Riots had been caused by Jews at the instigation of a 'Chrestus'. It seems probable that the quarrels among the Jews were over the question whether the crucified Jesus was indeed the Messiah, the Christ. So the new faith will have been proclaimed to Christians of Jewish descent in Rome round about the year 49.

Probably Claudius expelled only the activists in both parties. In that case Aquila and Priscilla would belong among those who openly acclaimed Jesus as Messiah. For although Luke does not say so explicitly, they must have been Christians, otherwise Paul would certainly not have found accommodation and work with them.

As long as Paul had to earn his living, he could only go to the synagogue to preach and discuss on the sabbath. There was a change when Timothy and Silas arrived from Macedonia. It seems that they brought contributions from the Christians there, probably from Philippi. This gave Paul more elbow room and he could devote himself completely to preaching.

After the arrival of the two men, Paul sent his letter to the Christians in Thessalonica. Perhaps he dictated it in the house of Titius Justus, a God-fearer, who according to Luke lived next to the synagogue and responded to Paul's preaching. This man with a Latin name evidently had a large house, with a room in which Paul could receive people in peace throughout the week. So this early convert was a well-to-do citizen.

Luke also mentions a certain Crispus, who attached himself to Paul. He was a Jew and a wealthy one at that. He held the post of 'overseer of the synagogue'. He was responsible not only for supervising liturgical services, readings from the scriptures, prayers and sermons, but also for looking after the structure of the building. Because of this, people usually chose prosperous Jews for the post, so that if necessary they could contribute to needs out of their own pockets.

A few years later, Paul was to mention in his letters other Corinthian Christians from the early days who had a 'house': this meant not only a dwelling, but also a household which would doubtless have included servants and slaves. They were therefore wealthy citizens who put their possessions at the disposal of the Christian community, and were also in constant touch with Paul, to support him wherever he was.

Crispus, the overseer of the synagogue, was baptized by Paul himself, as was a certain Gaius, and also Stephanas. But according to his own account Paul usually left the work of baptism to others, his fellow-workers, who also saw to the preparation for it.

Later on, when Paul is writing from Corinth to the Christians in Rome, he sends them greetings from Gaius, who was mentioned in the last paragraph. Evidently he was staying with him since he calls him 'my host and the host of the whole Christian community'.

There were greetings too from Erastus, whom Paul describes as city treasurer. This must have been a very important post in the administration of Corinth. Finally, a certain Tertius adds his greeting; he must have been an educated man, because Paul dictated the letter to the Romans to him.

So the new group in Corinth did not just consist of unlettered people, dock-workers and paupers. It reflected the great social differences which according to ancient writers were characteristic of Corinth: very rich men and very poor men side by side.

This explains some of the tensions and conflicts in the Christian community, in which Paul was to be involved a few years later. But above all, it answers a question which often comes up whenever I go through Paul's letters with Bible groups: 'Weren't his letters far too difficult for simple unlettered Christians?' The answer is 'No', because the leading figures in the young communities were well educated. They are also mostly the Christians whom we know by name. That tells us a good deal. Paul will have talked with the leaders in Corinth a lot during his year and a half there. They will have been well aware of his concerns. Indeed, they had become so familiar with the essence of Paul's message and its consequences that they could talk about it and live it out in their own way. They regarded themselves as independent Christians, able to pass judgment on other ways of believing and living, in the end even on Paul's way.

As a climax to the story of Paul's activity in Corinth, Luke describes how the Jews brought him before the judgment seat of Gallio, the proconsul. However, this Roman did not want to pronounce any verdict in what he felt to be a domestic Jewish matter.

The mention of Gallio gives us a point of reference for dating Paul's visit. The Roman probably took up his post as proconsul over the province of Achaea in May AD 51. If the accusation by the Jews took place shortly after that, and towards the end of Paul's eighteen months' stay, then Paul must have arrived in Corinth at the beginning of 50 and left at the end of 51.

He seems to have wanted to return to his base in Antioch. From Corinth there were regular ships to Ephesus, the famous metropolis of Asia Minor on the other side of the Aegean. The sailors of the time liked to keep the coast in sight as much as possible, and they could do this on the route because there were so many islands. Paul went to Ephesus with Aquila and Prisca, the Jewish couple, who evidently wanted to move there. After that he took a ship bound for Antioch. Perhaps it was an unfavourable wind that made him land at Caesarea, on the coast of Palestine. From the way in which he writes about it in his two books, the Gospel and Acts, Luke seems to have cherished some affection for the city, so perhaps that is why he mentions Paul's visit there. It was not important. From there Paul went on to Antioch.

—⊃ 7 ⊂—

From Ephesus to Galatia

Luke does not tell us what Paul did in Antioch. He simply says that 'after some time' Paul left the city again on a new journey. This was in the spring (of 52 or 53), when the snow had melted on the Taurus mountains. The journey was in the direction of Ephesus, but via the communities in the interior of Asia Minor. Paul travelled through 'the land of Galatia' for the second time and through Phrygia, and then arrived at Ephesus.

Ephesus was the chief city in Asia Minor. One might say that it was a kind of combination of Athens and Corinth, and more than that. For centuries it had been a centre of trade and culture. One of the first and greatest Greek philosophers, Heraclitus, came from Ephesus. Before Corinth was built, Ephesus had been a meeting place for east and west. People and merchandise came from the heart of Asia Minor and even further away, down the long river valley to the coastal city with its splendid situation in a fertile delta. Ships from the west came to berth in its secure harbour.

Down the ages, Ephesus had often been damaged by conquerors but on each occasion it rapidly recovered. The greatest attraction of the city lay in the worship of Artemis, the goddess who had come to embody all kinds of other fertility goddesses. She was a sort of earth mother. In the sixth century before Christ the legendarily rich king Croesus had had a temple built for her, and it was soon visited as one of the seven wonders of the world. In 356 BC a certain Herostratus set the temple on fire in an attempt to win worldwide notoriety. However, the enterprising Ephesians soon built a new one, which was even more splendid than the old.

The story that Luke tells in chapter 19 of his book about Paul's experiences in Ephesus is very compelling and dramatic. As in Corinth, Paul begins in the synagogue. The resistance of a number of Jews compels him to look for another room. This he found in the school of a certain Tyrannus, where he gave instruction every day for two years. Luke then describes the many miracles which Paul did, his victory over the Jewish exorcists and the public burning of valuable magical books. The climax of his sketch is the uproar caused by the silversmiths, who made little temples of Artemis and sold them to pilgrims; they now saw their trade collapsing because of the irresistible success of Paul's preaching. This is what Luke wants us to imagine. In his plan, Ephesus is the scene of Paul's last achievements in an international city before his arrest.

In fact, Paul did not feel that the progress of his work had been quite as triumphant as that. On the contrary, during the years in Ephesus he had worked hard, toiled and suffered; he had even been put in prison, and for a long time he had not known whether he would ever get out again. We know something of all this from the letters which he sent from Ephesus that have survived. In one of them he cannot resist summing up the hardships and dangers of his life as an apostle. On several occasions he had been flogged and beaten with sticks, he had been involved in shipwrecks, and had undergone all kinds of dangers on his travels. He speaks of his slaving away, his sleepless nights, the hunger and cold which he had to put up with; then he goes on to say: in addition to all these things from outside, day in and day out there is 'my care of all the churches'. The letters from Ephesus bear witness to this. But before we go into them more deeply it will perhaps be a good thing to discuss a couple of features of Paul's view of his work.

First of all Paul finds it unthinkable that anyone can be a believer on his own. To believe in Christ is essentially to join a group which lives 'in Christ', a group which is based on Christ and permeated by his life. Of course the language here is metaphorical.

Sometimes Paul speaks about such a community of Christians as though they were a building, a house or dwelling. Then he says that Christ is its 'foundation'. Following this imagery, one might say that such a group is based on Christ. But the comparison with a building is inadequate, because the community is alive. So Paul prefers to speak in terms of an organism, a body. To be a Christian is to be a member of the living body, which he sometimes calls 'the body of Christ', and sometimes just 'Christ'. For Paul, this description indicates both the one person of Jesus and the other human persons who are affected by him, united with him in such a way that his life is also theirs. So following Paul's imagery, one might say that the community is permeated by the life of Christ.

When Paul has in mind the nature and quality of lives that are now fulfilled by Christ, and the power that streams from him (the language is still, of course, metaphorical) into the believers who are united with him, he is fond of using the old biblical term spirit, breath. This is clearly a reference to the way in which God the Creator breathes life into his creatures. The Spirit breathed new life into the Christ who died on the cross to such a boundless degree that he can pass it on to all those who entrust themselves to him and believe in him. They are then filled with the new life of the Spirit.

It is difficulty for us cold-blooded northerners, inheritors of a Christianity which is somewhat the worse for wear, to imagine ourselves caught up in the reality which was so obvious to Paul. When groups of Christians formed after hearing him preach they often experienced the breath of God, the Spirit, very vividly in their meetings. They felt 'inspired'.

But whenever men share an enterprise or a belief, friction eventually develops. Even in these inspired communities, misunderstandings and quarrels arose; one person seemed a little more inspired than his neighbour, and then the neighbour discovered that there was more to the new life than enthusiasm . . . As long as Paul was still around, he could do something about this. He helped people to achieve the peace and harmony which must characterize any Christian community. He was better than anyone else at explaining what really mattered, and was good at making rules for meetings and personal relationships and dealings with outsiders. They worked, because when all was said and done he was the founder of the group. His words had as it were brought the group to life; he could call himself (again metaphorically) the 'father' of the community. This gave him a unique authority because no one else could talk like this.

Once Paul had gone off to found a Christian community somewhere else, the group had to go on without him. But Paul maintained contact with them; we have already seen how colleagues kept him up to date on what was happening in Thessalonica and how he also stayed in touch by writing letters. He told them that he was alive and well and indeed had been encouraged to hear that Christians were standing fast in the Lord and living in the strength of Christ.

In Paul's view that was no exaggeration. The growth of the 'body of Christ' was a matter of life and death for him. It affected his whole being. Hence his agitation whenever he heard that a particular group was no longer living 'in the Spirit', and that its members were no longer wholly 'in Christ'. Hence, too, his heartfelt expressions of thanks whenever he heard that all was going well.

Paul's agitated way of talking, his passion, the way in which he and his churches experienced the Spirit, are reminders that he and the people to whom he was writing lived around the Mediterranean. Anyone who has been on holiday in Spain, Portugal, Italy, Greece or North Africa, and has really come into contact with the people there, will be familiar with the Latin temperament and should remember it whenever they read Paul.

I have hesitated over which of Paul's letters from Ephesus I should begin with. I have chosen the one to the Galatians, although there is dispute whether this (along with other letters) was in fact sent from there, and although I have sympathy with the view that Paul wrote it when he had already left Ephesus and was on his way to Macedonia. Still, it seems to me a very good way of getting to know Paul. It is all of a piece, and anyone who reads it thoughtfully can feel Paul's presence, with all his emotions, his fury, his sense of personal injury and at the same time his passionate love for the people in Galatia.

What was the trouble with the Galatians? And who were they,

anyway? People often express surprise when they hear that the Galatians are the same people as our Celts. I then tell them how a number of tribes from this very old and dynamic people from central Europe appeared in the Balkans some centuries before Christ. A prince from Asia Minor then hired three of them to fight for him as mercenaries. They did that and became his subjects: the wild Celts wandered around for years robbing and plundering until they finally came to settle in the centre of Asia Minor, in the region of what is now Ankara. The Romans subjugated them and were glad to make use of these new 'confederates' in their military enterprises. However, none of this is really important for our understanding of Paul's letter.

It does, however, seem a good thing to ask how Paul came to be in the interior of Asia Minor and why he founded communities there. After all, this was not on his itinerary. From notes which Luke has incorporated into his narrative, and which are certainly old, it seems that at the beginning of his second journey Paul really wanted to go into the coastal province of Asia, of which Ephesus was the capital. However, for one reason or another he could not manage this, so he went through the region of Galatia and through Phrygia, with the intention of reaching Bithynia. His aim is quite understandable. Bithynia was on the coast of the Black Sea, and like nearby Pontus it had a number of flourishing harbours. For Paul, therefore, these were promising cities, centres from which his message could spread across the enormous inland sea, to Russia and the Balkans. It is worth considering how Christianity might have developed had Paul gone in that direction and not to Greece.

But here again, we have no firm facts to go on. Luke has obviously omitted to mention some places so as to bring Paul to Greece as soon as possible. Moreover, in Acts 16, like a true biblical historian, he makes the Holy Spirit the real force behind Paul's journey. This does not help anyone who is looking for information.

In his letter to the Galatians he refers to his first visit to them. However, it is difficult to see precisely what he means:

You did not wrong me in any way. You know that I first

preached the gospel to you because of a weakness of the flesh, and though my condition was a trial for you, you did not despise me or reject me. You received me as an angel of God, as Christ Jesus himself.

Later on he says:

You were so pleased with me that if possible you would have plucked out your eyes and given them to me.

Here we have a case where Paul knew precisely what he was referring to, and his readers could understand it immediately, whereas we are confronted with riddles. What does he mean by this 'weakness of the flesh'? Why was he a 'trial' to the Galatians? Why were they so ready to give him their eyes? Many commentators think that Paul fell sick on his journey through Galatia and that during this enforced delay he could not refrain from preaching the gospel to his hosts, too. He also writes mysteriously in one of his letters to Corinth about something that torments him and thwarts him terribly, so much so that he confesses to having begged God three times to free him from it.

Numerous articles and books have been written by biblical scholars and by doctors, with all kinds of suggestions about the sickness which Paul may have suffered from. People have thought of various forms of falling sickness, epilepsy; attacks of hysteria which sometimes robbed him of his sight; very bad headaches; sciatica or some other kind of rheumatic pain; malaria; nightmares; depressive states; deafness; impediments of speech like stuttering; and even leprosy and other diseases have been suggested. However fascinating all the learned articles may be (where they are simple enough to be read by those who are not specialists in medicine), we are left with a riddle and reduced to guesswork. If Paul is referring to a sickness, then whatever it was, it must have been very troublesome for him. This was not just because it interfered with his travelling and his work as an apostle. One thought above all made it difficult to accept: how could God allow his Paul, whom he had chosen so unmistakably as the apostle to the non-Jews, to be tormented by an illness? He should at least have seen to it that his apostle was as fit as possible.

There was another thing which must have added immeasurably to Paul's distress. In the view of many Christians, including Paul himself, sickness was a sign that the renewing power of Christ still had not had its full effect on the believer. For Paul, sickness was anything but a good advertisement. I recently read this comment by an American scholar: 'A sick apostle is almost like a one-legged football player, a contradiction in terms, because sickness was really a sign of the powers of the old age at work to double-cross the work of God.' However, all this would arise only if Paul was indeed referring to a sickness in these obscure remarks, and it has to be said on the other side that all Paul's achievements presuppose a very strong constitution!

Paul does not mention any particular city in his letter to the Galatians, as he does in all his other letters. It perhaps follows from this that in Galatia he preached only in small places. This time it again amazes Paul that his preaching had a powerful effect on these simple people. That is surprising even now. The story of the one God and his crucified Son who would soon appear as judge, to bring justice to the poor and the oppressed and those without hope, had gripped the Galatians and made them almost mad with joy. Once again Paul had seen how the gospel could catch hold of people and make them new. Instead of being anxious and overburdened, feeling themselves oppressed by evil spirits, they became truly free men, with completely new perspectives on life and a new way of getting along together. The gospel really did have what might be called a saving power.

On his third journey, with Ephesus as his main destination, Paul had paid a flying visit to the Galatians, 'to strengthen the disciples', as Luke writes in chapter 18. At that time everything seems to have been going well. But towards the end of his stay in Ephesus, when his plans for a journey to Macedonia and Greece were fixed, he heard that something had gone wrong in Galatia, so wrong in fact that he regarded it as a disaster.

Christians, probably former Jews, had come there from outside and thrown the young communities into confusion. 'This new faith of yours', they said, 'is an illusion. It does not really bring you to the one true God. You know that he is the God of Israel, the God of the Jews. He is still allied only to them, and the sign of belonging in this alliance is circumcision. Only Jews have his revelation, the Torah, which was with him before creation and will remain with him for ever. If you want to enter into a relationship with that God and expect salvation from him in this life and in the life to come, then you must bear the sign of his covenant in your body. You must be circumcised, and you must live in accordance with his Torah, for example by paying special heed to the sabbath and by celebrating the great Jewish festivals.'

'But does all this apply now that God has sent his Messiah?', the Galatians asked. 'Yes', was the answer. 'Yes, it is now even clearer than before that he wants non-Jews to enter his covenant, and he wants them, the Gentiles, to live according to his will and his law.'

'But Paul never told us that we had to do all this.' 'No,' came the reply, 'of course not. Paul is not a real apostle. He was never one of those whom Jesus chose, who received their commission directly from him. Paul wants to be popular among the non-Jews. That is why he is making the way to God so easy. But this way does not lead to God. Paul ought to know that, because he is a Jew himself. So he had never understood properly, or he is a deliberate traitor . . .'

The Galatian Christians probably thought that the first comments, about circumcision and the law, were very sensible. To belong to God by virtue of a clear token on one's body, and to live according to his laws, at least provided reassurance. You knew where you were. It was a sign of belonging. This was much clearer than Paul's talk about a God who loves you and sends his Spirit. It was also more human, for how is a man to give some direction to his life if he is not bound by fixed rites and customs? And of all the 'Eastern' religions which were on offer, Judaism was probably the most attractive.

When Paul heard of this he was very upset. In fact he was furious. How could so-called brothers in the faith have misled the simple people of Galatia, how could they have set them back so, and destroyed their freedom? And to think that at the same time they had denigrated him, Paul, as though he were not a proper representative of God! He would have liked to have set off for Galatia immediately. But he could not do that. So he dictated his letter to a colleague, and added a personal postscript on the last page. 'Letter' is not really a good word for what he wrote. It is much more a well-thought-out argument, or rather a defence, a passionate defence put forward by the accused on his own behalf and on behalf of his cause. Whenever I read the letter I am always surprised how someone with such deep feelings never for a moment wanders from the main point of his defence.

Paul comes straight to the point in the opening address. Normally it would be: 'Paul, an apostle, and all the brothers who are with me, to the Christian churches in Galatia, grace be to you and peace from God the Father and our Lord Jesus Christ.' However, the intruders claim that Paul is not a real apostle and that the coming of the Messiah, Christ, does not mark a break with the past: the world remains as it was and God is still committed to his Torah. It is the only means of contact between him and mankind. So Paul dictates the address as follows:

> From Paul, whose call to be an apostle did not come from man or by means of man, but from Jesus Christ and God the Father, who raised him from death. All the brothers who are here join me in sending greetings to the churches of Galatia: May God our Father and the Lord Jesus Christ give you grace and peace. In order to set us free from this present evil age Christ gave himself for our sins, in obedience to the will of our God and Father. To God be the glory forever and ever! Amen.

To follow the mention of God with a thanksgiving was very much a Jewish touch.

In all the other letters, an address like this would be followed by a thanksgiving to God for all that he had given to the Christians to whom Paul was writing. That does not happen here. Paul feels no gratitude, but only amazement and anger. How could they have allowed themselves to be so deceived!

We have already read the first part of the argument which follows, when we talked about what happened after Paul's conversion. He was commissioned to proclaim the Son of God to the Gentiles directly by God himself and not by men in Jerusalem. Three years later he got to know Peter there during a visit which lasted a fortnight. After that it was fourteen years before he went to Jerusalem again. The leading figures there acknowledged that Paul served the same Lord as they did: he did not require circumcision and other Jewish practices from a Gentile who came to believe in him.

We have also heard Paul's account of his sharp words to Peter in Antioch. Peter did not want to go on eating with Christians who had formerly been Gentiles. For him, too, the old Jewish regulations were more important than the new community in Christ. Paul felt this was a betrayal of the gospel. He tells the Galatians how fiercely he attacked Peter, but his remarks are aimed at the people who are now confusing the Galatian Christians. 'How can you try to force Gentiles to live as Jews?' So Paul enquired. We have no idea whether Peter gave a convincing explanation of his actions as his reply is not recorded. Now Paul comes to the important point. He sums it up like this: 'No man is ever justified by doing what the law demands, but only through faith in Christ Jesus.'

This view, and the arguments which follow from it, is difficult for many of us to understand. I suspect that the Galatian converts may very well have had the same feeling. In fact I think that here too Paul is not writing primarily for them, but through them to the intruders, who have come to commend their Jewish practices. These Jewish Christians think and argue in a Jewish way, and Paul can do the same thing.

At the same time, he feels that in the last resort he cannot prove that he is right. What gives him life cannot really be expressed in words, much less in arguments. For him, being a Christian is a matter of life and death, and will always remain so. It is all to do with the Son of God who, in his love for us, unconditionally involved himself in our hopeless situation so that he could change it from the inside. By doing this he has provided, in his person, a new point of contact with the living, life-giving God. The way in which the new Galatian Christians experienced the Spirit corresponds to Paul's own experience which he cannot put into words. It all happened to them when Paul brought them the message of the crucified Son of God: at that time they began to feel and know that their salvation, their future, lay in him. And they had this overwhelming experience before they had heard a word about circumcision and the Jewish Law.

Let me try to show in my own words how Paul explains and illustrates his own position. Before that, however, we must remember that when Paul speaks of the Torah, the Law, he can mean at least two different things. He can either be referring to the book of the Torah, as the first part of the Old Testament, or he can be thinking of the commandments which are said in that book to have been given by God to his people on Sinai. Jewish tradition developed these commandments into a code of law with which the number 613 was always connected. There were said to be 613 commandments and prohibitions.

Paul takes as his starting point the self-confident Jewish attitude familiar to Peter and the Jewish Christians who had come to Galatia: 'We are Jews by birth and not sinners from among the Gentiles.' Someone who had been born a Jew belonged to God and stood in the covenant relationship with him. He was righteous, whereas all non-Jews were by nature 'sinners'; they stood outside the covenant with the one God and were idolaters, enemies of God.

Now the Jew lived out his relationship with God, and thus his own 'righteousness', by keeping God's commandments and doing 'the works of the Law'. That is all very well, says Paul, but when you entrust yourself and your future to Christ, the new point of contact, through whom God involves you in a relationship with himself, you confess that doing the works of the Law is not enough. In other words, you will realize that your relationship with God had been broken, so that you were really in the same position as the Gentiles. Even as a Jew, you were far from God, a 'sinner', and hostile to him.

Paul seems to mean that every Jew is really in this position. For once somebody has transgressed even one of the 613 regulations, he has broken his relationship with God, forfeited all claims to 'righteousness' and has become a sinner. However well he observes all the other commandments, in other words, however well he does 'the works of the Law', he can never restore his broken relationship with God. Only God can do that, by a gesture from his side. And that is what he has done in Christ. Only by accepting this offer, by believing, is it possible to regain that relationship with God, to cease to be a 'sinner' and to become righteous.

Once Paul has reminded the Galatians of the overwhelming experience they had to begin with, of the way in which they were gripped by the Spirit, he goes on to give an elaborate picture of Abraham. It is not just elaborate; one might say that it is extremely concentrated. It seems as though the reports from Galatia had set him thinking very hard. Flashes of intuition come one after the other. Biblical sayings are put in a new context, and he combines them in an attempt to show the completely new possibilities which have been opened up by the death of Christ.

The discussion begins with Abraham, and Paul works with a series of contrasting terms: blessing/curse, faith/fulfilling of the Law, life/death. He also brings in the Torah both as a Law book and as the story of God's dealings with men and his plans for them.

After announcing numerous commandments and prohibitions, the Law book says: 'Anyone who does not keep all the commandments in this book of the Law is cursed.' Now one of the commandments in the Law decrees that an executed man who is hung on a stake must be buried the same day. If his corpse were to hang overnight, the land would be defiled. For the commandment says: 'Anyone who hangs on a tree is cursed'. Now Paul combines these two statements in the Torah about a curse and arrives at the following conclusion: Christ has taken upon himself the curse which the Law pronounces over those who transgress it, the 'sinners', because he has died on a cross and so has himself become accursed. By doing this he has freed those who stand under the curse of the Law so that they can live in the completely new relationship to God which can be found in the person of Christ himself.

Now the Torah, seen as a story, describes how Abraham believed that God accepted him as a righteous man. This way of believing was to be offered as a possibility to all peoples. According to Paul, this had already been announced in the promise to Abraham: 'In you all the peoples shall be blessed.' So the experience of the Galatians, the way in which they accepted Paul's message in faith and received the spirit, were fully in accordance with God's real, original plan.

Paul compares the promise to Abraham and his 'seed' with a will, God's testament. Anyone who reads the Torah as a narrative will see that the proclamation of the Law on Sinai came about 430 years after the promise. Of course the Law was also instituted by God, but it did not annul the original decree, God's testament. The 'seed' of Abraham, in whom God was to fulfil his promise (i.e. Christ and those who believe in him) was not to appear until well into the future, so the Torah was necessary as a Law, an emergency measure.

Paul attacks Jewish views quite strongly when he stresses that character of the Torah. Jews may claim that the Torah existed before creation and will remain until heaven and earth pass away. But that is hardly the case. It was given 430 years after Abraham, as an emergency measure, and now that Christ has come it is abrogated. Moreover, the Torah was not given directly by God, but by means of angels and through Moses. It was really a second-hand revelation. It was also an emergency measure to keep Israel in check until the coming of Christ. It was a 'pedagogue' of the kind that Paul knew from his surroundings: a slave who was put in charge of children, who taught them manners in a rather heavy-handed way, and took them to school . . . Now, however, the regime of the Torah was finished. The pedagogue had been dismissed. For Paul, we have now become God's children. In Christ we are all on the same footing before God, and like Jesus we can dare to address him in our prayers with the affectionate cry 'Abba'.

I do not think that we should isolate Paul's 'biblical' arguments as they have been described above. If we do that, they may seem artificial. He framed them with an eye to the Galatians, and above all with an eye to those who wanted to impose the Torah on Christians. He himself probably felt that his arguments were rather incoherent. He was essentially a mystic, a man who had been touched by God. His experience near Damascus must have been something like a divine kiss, a powerful, if not fatal embrace. It was fatal for the Paul who had identified himself with the regime of the Torah, but at the same time it freed him for a love which was not deterred by the cross, the worst fate that could happen. His old self, which had become one with that system, was now dead, so the system was dead for him, too. At the same time a new life had dawned for him which he associates with the name of Christ. His life now consisted in faith, trust, surrender to the one who had appeared to him near Damascus, and who would never let him go.

Hence his reference to the experience the Galatians had had with him. It was because he was obviously called by God and therefore totally devoted to them, completely at their disposal, that he could also pass on the story of God's love to them effectively. Furthermore, the Spirit had played its part in making them open to others. So the Galatians for their part could trust Paul completely, seeing that he had proved to be so manifestly Christ's representative. Such an experience of mutual trust works in quite a different way from arguments.

Is Paul then reverting to the level of argument when he starts with Abraham all over again, this time talking about Abraham's two sons and their mothers? I think not. He seems, rather, to be trying to describe what he sees now: two groups of people and two communities. One type arises wherever people are moved by the gospel and the Spirit of God renews them from within. The Spirit frees them from all their former anxieties and from whatever set them at odds with one another: Jew and Gentile, slave and free man, man and woman now come together in this totally new pattern of life. Paul sees a great contrast between this new community and the Jews, who are kept together by a covenant which has circumcision as an outward sign and the Torah as a rule of life.

Now the Bible often represents a group of people, a nation, as a woman. Israel is often called the bride of God or God's spouse. Sometimes the same metaphor is used for the capital of a country or a people. Babylon is described as a whore, as is Jerusalem when its inhabitants have been unfaithful to their God. Jesus, too, addressed the city of Jerusalem as a woman, and its inhabitants as her children: 'How often have I wanted to gather your children together . . .' This explains how Paul can picture the new community as another Jerusalem, the heavenly Jerusalem. It has been called into being by the Spirit of God, and its children continually increase. The heavenly Jerusalem is contrasted with the earthly Jerusalem, the centre of Judaism, which is in captivity and lives under the constraints of the Law. This earthly Jerusalem is a great trial to the new community in Christ, which it persecutes.

I suppose that it was while he was thinking in biblical terms about the Galatian Christians and the trouble-makers that Paul remembered the two wives of Abraham, the man whom he had mentioned earlier in his letter. One of them was a free woman, Sarah. She was barren for a long time, so Abraham had a son by her slave-girl Hagar. This son, too, was a slave. He and his mother were driven into the wilderness. Now the wilderness lay around the foot of Sinai, the scene of the giving of the Torah which held the Jews captive . . . Paul also knows the Jewish tradition which records that Hagar's son (Ishmael) imposed on Sarah's child (Isaac) and persecuted him, which is why he and his mother were driven out. In this remarkable passage he seems to be trying to say, 'Do you see the point, Galatians? Those who want to force you to be circumcised and to obey the Torah to the letter are slaves. If you listen to them you will be giving up your existence as free men to live in slavery. So take the hint and drive these men away.'

This may have been confusing and obscure for the Galatians, but for the Jews it was downright offensive. They were proud of their descent from Abraham through Isaac, the son of the promise. The son of Hagar was the ancestor of the Arabians. Here Paul claims true 'descent' from Abraham for the new community in the Spirit and portrays the Jewish people as Ishmael, the son of the slave-girl. When I realize how offensive Paul is there to Jewish self-esteem, I am inclined to ask him, 'Paul, do you have to be like that . . .'

When he was referring to the danger that the Galatians might revert to an acceptance of the Jewish Law, Paul remarked, 'You began with the spirit and now you are going to end with the flesh!' He often uses the nouns 'flesh' and 'spirit', and also the adjectives 'fleshly' and 'spiritual', especially in the last part of this letter. But he does not mean by them what the English words suggest.

When Paul talks about 'the desires of the flesh', some people think of a taste for good food and drink and sex: what are sometimes called our baser instincts. Spiritual matters are associated with the higher parts of our nature, the head and the heart. But Paul does not think like this. He does not recognize a distinction between different elements in human nature. For him it is quite possible that a celibate scholar might live 'according to the flesh', while a lover of food, drink and sex could live 'in the spirit'.

Paul's use of 'flesh' and 'spirit' goes back to the Old Testament. I think that the great prophet Isaiah, the prophet of faith, was the first to use the words in this sense. Because the king of Jerusalem was anxious about the Assyrian threat from the north, he entered into an alliance with the Egyptians in the south, who had a strong force of chariots. In chapter 31 of the book of Isaiah we read how the prophet condemned this defensive alliance, remarking tersely:

> Egypt is man and not God,
> their horses are flesh and not spirit . . .

In chapter 40 of the same book, another prophet proclaims freedom from Babylonian captivity. This seems an impossibility, since Babylon has the upper hand. But appearances are deceptive, says the prophet, since all their glory and power is only flesh, as transitory as a flower in the summer wind. As before, the term 'flesh' is used to denote the human state common to all mankind, and it is frequent in the Old Testament after this.

'Flesh' characterizes human existence as transitory, mortal and weak. It is often also used with moral connotations: men are weak in obedience and trust towards God and each other, and so are really sinful.

During the last two centuries before Christ, persecuted Jews began to expect that 'this (evil) world' would be replaced by a 'world to come'. Along with this expectation went a way of thinking in black and white which can often be found among people who feel crushed and desperate. Because they have no hope, they direct their thoughts to a completely new world order. We have seen how Paul shared the Jewish expectation and how because of this background he too thought in strongly contrasting terms. He saw things this way not least because he had experienced such a complete conversion in his own life. He felt the power of the 'world to come' already at work in his own life and saw its effect where his message struck home. There the Spirit was at work in the new creation which had been begun in Christ.

Paul often uses 'flesh' to describe human existence which has not yet been touched by the Spirit. It is transitory, subject to death, without prospects, even sinful, cut off from God and therefore at war with him. Because there is only black or white, there can be no grey. When it comes to matters of life and death, no man can be neutral.

Human existence, characterized by sin and death, is also beset by all kinds of hostile powers and forces in the universe. Men feel oppressed by these forces and try to ward them off by all sorts of religious practices. But their attempts, too, are always 'fleshly': they are powerless and sinful, and fail to open up the way to the living God and his lifegiving Spirit.

But a way has been opened up for the Galatians who have listened to the gospel and been gripped by the Spirit. However, if they now accept circumcision and the Torah, they will lapse into the world of the flesh. So Paul puts Jewish religion as propagated by those who trouble the Galatian Christians on the same level as the pagan religion from which the Galatians had themselves been rescued. He may seem to be putting it strongly, but that is understandable in an emotional plea. Some time later, in the calmer argument which he addresses to the Romans, he will speak in rather more considered terms.

In the admonitions at the end of the letter, Paul gives a list of vices, examples of bad conduct, and after that a list of virtues. Such summaries of sometimes twenty or thirty vices and virtues were frequent in the moralizing literature of his time. The way in which Paul introduces the series is typical. He describes bad conduct as 'the works of the flesh', what man does because he is weak and sinful: 'immorality, impurity, licentiousness, idolatry, sorcery, enmity, strife, jealousy, anger, selfishness, dissension, envy, drunkenness, carousing and the like.' He contrasts all this with a list of positive virtues which he introduces with the phrase 'the fruit of the spirit', in the singular. This fruit is in the first place love, and it is followed by what might be called the symptoms of love: 'joy, peace, long-suffering, friendliness, goodness, trust, gentleness, self-control.'

Laws were given to keep in check man's wickedness, the works 'of the flesh'. Where the Spirit has taken hold of people, love flourishes from within and the law is no longer necessary.

I have described the letter as Paul's defence. By that I really mean a speech in which a plaintiff defends a case in public. Anyone studying to be a barrister must make himself familiar with the construction and style that such a speech must have. The construction and style of a speech for the defence differs from, say, that of a sermon or an election speech.

In Paul's time the greater part of education was devoted to the use of language, to oratory. We even have some textbooks about it which have survived from classical times. In our day scholars are reading them again to see how far New Testament writings correspond to the textbook rules. Paul's letter to the Galatians does, in fact, seem to have the structure of a defence speech. As an example, let me say something about the requirements put forward by the best authorities for the conclusion to such a speech.

The important thing is to convince the judge or jury. The end of the speech must present the essential points once again in a highly emotional way. At the same time the speaker must refer back to the beginning of his argument. Furthermore, he must put his opponents firmly in their place, make them seem so ridiculous that even the jury has no patience with them. Finally, he must gain sympathy for his cause and, if possible, sympathy for himself or the defendant for whom he pleads. The personal conclusion which Paul adds in his own handwriting certainly seems to fulfil all these conditions.

The jury was made up of the Christians of Galatia. The prosecution consisted of the Jewish Christians who were arguing that the 'fleshly' rite of circumcision was the only way of getting into other peoples' good books. That was a 'fleshly' reason if ever there was one! Paul argues that his opponents are dishonest and cowardly, fearful for the consequences of the cross, which call for a complete break with the world of the flesh. Those who accept these consequences become new men from within, with new inspiration and a new set of motives and perspectives. At the beginning of his letter Paul pronounced a curse on those who proclaimed another gospel. Now he returns to this highly authoritative manner of speaking, but this time in the form of a blessing on those who live according to the one true gospel and on the Israel of God. Perhaps by this last phrase he means the Jewish people who are still looking for their Messiah: although they utterly reject Jesus, that is infinitely better than to be as half-hearted as the so-called Christian propagandists in Galatia.

Finally Paul seeks the sympathy of the jury. He does not want them to feel sorry for him, but he does want them now, once and for all, to decide in favour of the cause which he defends. They must not make him anxious all over again. His loyalty to that cause involved him in torture, the scars of which are still visible on his body. However, that is not a reason for pitying him: his wounds are proof that he really is presenting the crucified Lord and appearing in his name.

You see these big letters? I am now writing to you in my own hand. It is all those who want to make a fair outward and bodily show (in the flesh) who are trying to force circumcision upon you: their sole object is to escape persecution for the cross of Christ. For even those who do receive circumcision are not thoroughgoing observers of the law; they only want you to be circumcised in order to boast of your having submitted to that outward rite. But God forbid that I should boast of anything but the cross of our Lord Jesus Christ, through which the world is crucified to me and I to the world! Circumcision is nothing: uncircumcision is nothing: the only thing that counts is new creation! Whoever they are who take this principle for their guide, peace and mercy be upon them, and upon the whole Israel of God! In future let no one make trouble for me, for I bear the marks of Jesus branded on my body.

— 8 —

To his Friends in Philippi

After the fierce and concentrated argument addressed to the Galatians, I was glad to turn to Paul's letter to the Philippians. Here were people who caused him no trouble. On the contrary, the very fact that they were so anxious about his welfare proved their concern for him. The community in Philippi was the only one from which he accepted financial support, and for Paul that is saying something.

The community was his first love in Europe. Having crossed over from Troas to Macedonia, he began his work in Philippi, a city named after its founder King Philip, the father of Alexander the Great. The city was built in a favourable position, with the great Roman road, Via Egnatia, running past it. The Emperor Augustus had elevated it to the status of a Roman colony.

Luke tells some fascinating stories in Acts 16 about Paul's work in Philippi. They include some remarkable miracles. The first person to be converted was Lydia, a 'God-fearer', a business woman who dealt in purple fabric. That must have been a flourishing trade in Philippi, with so many Roman soldiers who wanted to wear purple. We also hear how Paul cast out an oracular spirit from a Gentile slave-girl, and how the governor of the prison accepted the faith, along with his whole household, and was baptized.

Were these people characteristic of the social composition of the Christian community as a whole? In any event, Paul's preaching must have had a good deal of success. He himself writes from Corinth to Thessalonica about the 'ill-treatment and the suffering' which he and his colleagues had endured in Philippi. This was always the other side of the coin: the founders

93

of the new, alien religious movement were persecuted, ill-treated and driven away.

However, the group experienced growth as well as persecution. They soon developed some degree of organization. This is clear from the 'address' in Paul's letter, which specially mentions 'episkopoi' and 'diakonoi' in the greeting to the Christians of Philippi. We have too little information to be able to describe the nature of these offices in more detail, but they were clearly held by leading figures.

When I read the letter to Philippi I usually begin at the end. The last section is an integral whole, a separate short letter, which is characteristic of Paul. We must remember that he is in prison in Ephesus, waiting for his case to come up. The guards seem to trust him and he is allowed to receive visitors and give letters to them, so that he can keep in touch with his Christian communities. He cannot, of course, earn his living, but he would very much like some money. Now the Christians of Philippi have sent one of their people, Epaphroditus, to him, with a financial contribution. Epaphroditus will also help in whatever way he can. Paul acknowledges their kindness with the letter we shall be looking at.

I do not imagine that the contribution from Philippi will have been very big. Paul could well have been content to write, 'Thank you, friends, the money will be very useful.' But no, he immediately sees the deeper significance of this small gesture, first of all for those who made it and then for himself, a man who wants to be a true apostle by relying only on his master and on no one else. This brief letter is not really a thank-you letter, then, except as thanks for the fact that the Philippians have so many benefits from their present!

It is a great joy to me in the Lord that now you have begun to show your care for me again — not that you did not care for me before, but you had no chance of showing it. Not that I am complaining of want, for I have learned to be self-sufficient in any situation.
I know how to be poor.
I know how to be rich.

I have been fully initiated into all aspects of human life: having plenty and being hungry, having more than I need and not having enough. I have strength to do anything through the one who gives me power.

We saw earlier why Paul made a point of never taking money from the people among whom he worked. Evidently he had often pondered whether this was the right decision, so here his thoughts come out in almost a poetic form. He had been 'initiated' into a variety of circumstances. To be 'self-sufficient', totally independent of anyone or anything else, was an ideal much cherished by the people of his time. In all his ups and downs, Paul had learnt that he could be independent through the power of one whose name he does not mention.

Then he talks to his people again. First he uses the language of bookkeeping. Their account is a good one, and it is well in credit. The actual term he uses is 'fruit', and this refers at the same time to the day of Christ's coming, which is so often pictured as the ingathering of a harvest. As he continues, Paul then goes over completely to the biblical language of sacrifice, and at the end shows again how everything begins with God and comes about through him.

But it was very good of you to help me in my troubles. You Philippians yourselves know very well that when I left Macedonia, in the early days of preaching the Good News, you were the only church to help me; you were the only ones who shared my profits and losses. More than once, when I needed help in Thessalonica, you sent it to me. It is not that I just want to receive gifts; rather, I want to see profit added to your account. Here, then, is my receipt for everything you have given me – and it has been more than enough! I have all I need, now that Epaphroditus has brought me all your gifts. These are like a sweet-smelling offering to God, a sacrifice which is acceptable and pleasing to him. And my God, with all his abundant wealth in Christ Jesus, will supply all your needs. To our God and Father be the glory for ever and ever.

Paul will have given this letter to someone who was going to Philippi. Epaphroditus remained on hand in order to be able to help him, and he did so with great devotion. Unfortunately he became dangerously ill and almost died. The Christians in Philippi came to hear about it. When Epaphroditus had recovered, Paul sent him back with a letter in which he gave the Philippians an account of how things were with him and how his case was progressing. He also wanted to encourage the community to persevere in the course on which they had embarked, despite all resistance, in true Christian brotherhood (we have already discussed the 'address' of the letter with its references to 'episkopoi' and 'diakonoi').

In his thanksgiving to God Paul describes how the Philippians are involved in his work and in his concerns, and then he says:

> I pray that your love will keep on growing more and more, together with true knowledge and perfect judgment, so that you will be able to choose what is best.

We should really pause for a long time over any statement of this kind. For the words which are translated 'knowledge' and 'judgment' were common among philosophers of the time who thought about the right way for people to behave. Paul uses the expression 'choose what is best' elsewhere, in connection with the Jews who see this moral beginning in the Torah which has been given them by God. For Paul, the life of those who believe in Christ is not directed by an external law but by the love which God has placed in their hearts, the 'fruit of the Spirit', which motivates action from within. At the same time, it is a gift which has to be fed by regular prayer if it is to grow.

However, we would do better to pause over what Paul writes about his situation as a prisoner. Unfortunately we cannot tell why Paul was arrested and held pending trial. The Philippians will certainly have learnt the reason, from Epaphroditus and others. It can hardly have been Paul's 'propaganda' for the gospel, since other Christians were busily at work in the area. They seem to have had different opinions and different attitudes. Some were evidently not convinced that Paul was in prison simply because of his preaching. Had he then committed some criminal offence? As a result they dissociated themselves from him in their proclamation of the gospel. Paul regarded this as an attack on him and found it very painful. Nevertheless, the important thing is that Christ was preached, in whatever way, and Paul was glad about that. That was the purpose of his life — and perhaps of his death.

> Yes, and rejoice I will, knowing well that the issue of it all will be my deliverance, because you are praying for me and the Spirit of Jesus Christ is given me for support. For, as I passionately hope, I shall have no cause to be ashamed, but shall speak so boldly that now as always the greatness of Christ will shine out clearly in my person, whether through my life or through my death. For to me life is Christ, and death gain; but what if my living on in the body may serve some good purpose? Which then am I to choose? I cannot tell. I am torn two ways: what I should like is to depart and be with Christ; that is better by far; but for your sake there is greater need for me to stay on in the body. This indeed I know for certain: I shall stay, and stand by you all to help you forward and to add joy to your faith.

Paul's view of the world so often seems different from ours. Many of his ideas are alien to us. But here he speaks from a situation which does not seem tied to any particular picture of the world. He is stuck in prison. His case is up for consideration. One day or another someone may come in with the news that the judge has passed the death sentence on him. Paul looks death in the face. Now it is clear that when he attempted his difficult explanations, as in his discussion of 'flesh' and 'spirit', he was never concerned only with theory, a way of thinking, a philosophy, or anything of that kind. He was always trying to express something of his own faith so that he could share it with others who had similarly been called by God.

Within the horizon of the 'flesh', i.e. human existence seen in isolation, life and death are absolute opposites. Death is the inexorable end to human life. The person who dies gives up everything. He ceases to be whoever he once was.

In the sphere of the Spirit, life and death are no longer complete opposites. As Paul experiences it, life is essentially made up of relationships. At the centre is his relationship with Christ, i.e. Jesus of Nazareth, who is now so filled with divine life that death no longer has any power over him and he can involve others in this unimaginably new mode of existence. As a result, Paul has also entered into a relationship with all those others who have been led by God into the sphere of the Spirit.

Paul's life is shaped by the experience of all these relationships. If he dies, his relationship with Christ will become all-embracing; the prospect is so overwhelming that Paul would choose a death sentence in preference to freedom. But he has the gift of bringing his fellow men happiness in the same faith and the same experience of a shared life in relationship with Christ. It therefore seems to him better that he should occupy his life in this way.

'For me death is gain.' That is definitely the language of faith. Christ now fills Paul's life, and after his death will make it even fuller than before. It is the language of faith, expressing strictly personal feelings to other believers who are also beginning to see their own life and death in the same light, or at least are attempting to do so. It must have been heartening for the Philippians to hear Paul talking like this. The man who had preached Christ to them now seemed to be remaining steadfast even in the face of death.

As I have just said, Paul speaks the language of faith, which makes sense only to believers. It is almost impossible for outsiders to grasp, and may even seem to be nonsense. Perhaps thinking the unthinkable is a feature of Christian faith. Jesus invites people to do it, especially in his parables. If your thinking gets stuck in a rut, you will never be open either to God or to your fellow men. After Passover, Jesus' disciples continued where he had left off, but now they were thinking about him. He died on the cross and yet he lives. That was inconceivable – God had brought life into the gloomy domain beyond death.

I used the image of the squared circle in connection with Paul. He had to contemplate what was utterly unthinkable for him as a

Jew: God was not bound to his Torah. If Paul put that into words, other Jews would just not understand. He was speaking the language of faith or, as he would put it, the language of the Spirit.

He goes on in this vein to write to his friends and fellow-Christians in Philippi. As he passionately urges them to respect one another and not to be selfish, he gives a poetic description of the pattern of life to be seen in Christ Jesus. Here was man as he was originally meant to be, the perfect 'image' of God. Yet he 'humbled himself': in obedience to God he lived a human life in the shadow of death and died on a cross. Consequently God accorded him the highest status conceivable, in biblical language, 'a name above every name'.

Many scholars think that at this point Paul is quoting a hymn to Christ which he had heard in one of his communities. He himself may have added 'the death of a cross' to the phrase 'became obedient to death'. And perhaps he also added the conclusion, which says that this exaltation of Jesus is ultimately to the glory of God the Father.

If this suggestion is right, then we have another feature to add to our portrait of Paul. Although he was himself a master in handling the language of faith, he could gratefully take over the words of others when they seemed appropriate.

Once Paul has commended his colleague Timothy, and also Epaphroditus, he seems to be coming to the end of his letter. 'Finally, brothers, rejoice in the Lord . . .' But suddenly we discover that there are people around of the same stamp as the intruders in Galatia at whom Paul hurls words of abuse (dogs, evil workers, mutilators). These intruders refer to their privileges as Jews, to circumcision and the Torah, and think that this makes them 'complete Christians'. As a contrast to the attitude of these enemies of the cross of Christ, Paul then relates his own belief, and asks the Philippians to take him as their model.

After words of advice to particular people, he then goes back to his earlier mood with an invitation to rejoice: 'Rejoice in the Lord always, and again I say rejoice.' It has been suggested that the passage between the two invitations (chapter 3 and the beginning of chapter 4) comes from a later letter, written by Paul when he heard that his beloved community in Philippi was being threatened by 'heretical' propaganda.

Whether or not this is the case, in this passage we hear Paul talking about his 'conversion'. He mentions some of the privileges of which he was once so proud: 'Circumcised on the eighth day, Israelite by race, of the tribe of Benjamin, a Hebrew born and bred; in my attitude to the law, a Pharisee; in pious zeal, a persecutor of the church; in legal rectitude, faultless.' But when Paul came into contact with Christ, he regarded all these advantages as losses, indeed as 'so much garbage'. The only thing that mattered was to live in communion with Christ, and now he wants this communion to become deeper and deeper, so that he can share more in Christ's death in order to take part in his resurrection.

A great many Jews saw their obedience to the Torah as belonging within the context of the covenant: it was a real personal relationship with the God who had chosen them. Paul seems to have seen things in rather a different light. For him, Judaism was acceptance of a system which excluded the greater part of mankind, and indeed the majority of Jews. Did he long, deep down, for contacts and relationships with a wider community, and is this why he was so deeply affected by his encounter with Christ?

— 9 —

Paul to the Corinthians

From Ephesus, Paul also kept in contact with the community he had 'planted' in Corinth. The Christians there have preserved some of his letters, and originally there were more. The letter which is called the First Letter to the Corinthians in our Bible is not in fact the first, as it contains a reference to an earlier letter by Paul.

What fascinates me about the 'first' letter is that it shows us a church in the first flush of youth, a completely new group which is trying to get itself organized. In his unique role as 'founder', Paul offers help and gives instructions. Here we can see an unprecedented development which is taking place in a different culture from our own. We need a good deal of imagination to understand the unique situation.

Without doubt the most difficult thing for us to grasp is the Corinthians' experience of the 'Spirit'. While the Christians in the depths of Galatia were on the whole disturbed by the phenomenon, most of the converts in Corinth seem to have regarded experience of the Spirit as the essential feature of their new situation. They attached great value to the vivid expressions of it. That, they thought, was what Christianity should really consist of.

One way in which the Spirit showed itself was in making people feel taken out of themselves (in Greek *ek-stasis*, out of one's usual condition, our 'ecstasy'). When one of the Christians had this feeling he began to make incomprehensible noises, muttering as though he were drunk. This way of talking was thought to be divinely inspired, the language of the Spirit or of angels, from a higher world. Sometimes another Christian might feel that he could translate the sounds into comprehensible words and explain them.

The Corinthian Christians were extremely proud that the Spirit was at work in them in such an unmistakable way. But this also gave rise to all kinds of tensions. Those who did not have this experience of 'speaking with tongues' might feel that they were second-class Christians. Perhaps these were the more rational types, the 'intellectuals'. But they had an opportunity to give a lucid account of the new faith and all that it involved. When this happened, they too seemed to be divinely inspired, with an authority like that of Christ himself. They found that as they gave advice and encouragement the Lord touched the hearts of members of the community through them. They called this 'prophesying'. And sometimes a person had the gift of penetrating the secret thoughts and feelings of another. This, too, was regarded as experience of the Spirit.

Enthusiasm (the Greek word means being filled with a deity) led the Christians to do a great deal more. Other remarkable things happened in the community. People were suddenly cured of illnesses, or had the urge to give away all their goods; they expressed their utter devotion to the cause of Christ; they were without the slightest fear of death, and so on.

Some were so caught up in the atmosphere of the community that they felt that they were in heaven The important thing was this ecstasy, which brought release from one's narrow-mindedness and cramped life-style. Paul had always spoken about resurrection as a future event. But the Corinthians thought that he was really referring to their present experience, a 'spiritual' resurrection from the old past.

These were startling new prospects; liberation from one's old self, the experience of a totally new community, a new union. Some Christians saw a connection between spiritual ecstasy and the ecstasy experienced in sexual intercourse. This was not so strange in their culture. It did not matter very much to them whether they experienced it within marriage or outside it. Indeed, in the new freedom, old customs and laws were no longer valid: anything was allowed. What you did with your body could have no effect on your new inner nature: that had been filled with the Spirit.

Other Christians did not see things this way. On the contrary, they felt that in the new spiritual situation purely physical relationships were not appropriate at all, and that if your spouse did not see things this way, you should take a very firm line. This led on to a particularly important question – did it make any difference whether or not your spouse had also become a believer and had entered the community of the Spirit?

We must use our imagination even more to understand another point discussed by the Corinthians, namely, the eating of meat. There were many temples in Corinth. Illustrated books and postcards from friends on holiday around the Mediterranean have made us very familiar with the Greek temples. Coloured photographs show them to be very impressive ruins. But the photographs also show them to be dead buildings. At the time when hordes of people came to them to pray and to offer sacrifices, the temples did not look so attractive. They were crowded, full of smoke and very smelly, because temples like this were really enormous abattoirs: cattle and smaller animals were killed as though on a production line, and almost all the meat from the animals went to the market.

Some Christians felt that they should not eat this meat. It had been offered to the gods and therefore really belonged to them; when you ate it, you were in fact a guest of the deity. Christians ought to give up this sort of thing. Moreover, since you were a renegade, the deity might well turn ugly on you. So even if you were at a family party, as a Christian you had to let the meat course go by.

No, said other Christians: we have come to know the one true God. We can see that the gods whom we once worshipped and feared do not exist at all. They are nobodies and can do nothing. Let yourself be guided by insight and knowledge, and not by fear! In any case, we shall not let our behaviour be affected by your qualms of conscience. Meat offered to the gods is no different from any of the other meat we eat. End of discussion.

There were yet other causes of tension. We have already seen that the Christians of Corinth included a number of well-to-do citizens. They put their possessions at the service of the community. They made use of their business trips to contact Paul. They also used their experience of business administration to organize the new communities. They could even offer accommodation to Christians from elsewhere who had more to teach them and who wanted to spend some time in Corinth. At this point I am thinking of Apollos. According to Luke in Acts 18, he must have been an exceptional person. He was a Jew from Alexandria, well-educated and eloquent, and steeped in the scriptures. Now that he had become a Christian he could talk about Jesus 'with great enthusiasm'. Luke mentions him first in Ephesus, but before Paul arrived there on his third journey, Apollos had moved to Corinth.

We can understand why some Corinthian Christians would be very much attracted by the figure of Apollos. As an orator he had more to offer than Paul, and with his thorough education in the Bible and philosophy his sermons would also have been more profound. Whenever Apollos plumbed the depths of a biblical text or a saying of Jesus, he will have been very impressive indeed. What a privilege to be able to support this man and give him lodging, and to entertain brothers and sisters who wanted to listen to him and talk with him in one's own house!

Christians from Jerusalem also came on visits. Conversation with them would open up prospects which Paul had never seemed to offer. The people from Jerusalem could say a good deal about Jesus, his life and his teaching. They could repeat sayings of Jesus, the wisdom of the master himself. And they had Peter's authority behind them. This man had originally been called Simeon, but Jesus had given him the name 'rock'. The Lord had made him the foundation of his new community. The Greek translation of the name was 'Peter', so this is what Greek-speaking Christians preferred to call the former Simeon. But it seems that the Corinthians who entertained the Christians from Jerusalem preferred the Aramaic form of the name, Cepha (which became Cephas with the addition of an s, which was essential for Greeks). It was a strange word and had a mysterious feel to it, a sound of its own; it seemed to provide a link with that distant land where everything had begun, and thus with the 'historical' Jesus. The 'rock man' who had been appointed by

Jesus himself and knew better than anyone else what Jesus had really said and meant provided a tangible foundation; one's faith did not hang in the air, as it did with Paul.

However, other Corinthians had different views. We are concerned with now, the present, they said, with the Lord as he is now and with the Holy Spirit which works so powerfully in us. And we owe that to Paul, who is himself so completely filled with this Spirit. To hell with what happened twenty-five years ago in distant Palestine! That is in the past, a fleeting series of events which can provide no real foundation. No one can experience *that* any more.

While Paul was having such a difficult time in Ephesus (as he remarks, in language reminiscent of the psalms, he had 'to fight with wild beasts' there), he received information from Corinth. We have already seen that there were regular sailings between the two cities. A certain married woman called Chloe reported to him through members of her household, or perhaps through business colleagues, that factions had formed round the persons of Peter, Apollos and Paul: some claimed to have better knowledge of the faith than others. Christians were also acting immorally on the basis of their new feeling of freedom: one man was even living with his stepmother! Others had accused one another of cheating in business affairs and had appeared before the court in Corinth. Christians were meeting in the houses of rich men, and their eucharists were too much like society dinners: distinguished guests had more than enough to eat and the poor went short.

In addition to these oral reports Paul also received a letter from Corinth asking a number of questions. What should be the relations between men and women in the new life of the Spirit? What dealings should Christians have with non-believers, especially when it came to eating meat? If we are really one with Christ through baptism and the eucharist, and know from experience that we live in the Spirit, then what is the meaning of a physical resurrection in the future?

Paul would much have preferred to take the fastest ship to Corinth. But he could not do that. So he did the two next best things. He gave instructions to Timothy, who was to go by land to Corinth via Macedonia, and he sat down and dictated a long epistle which he planned to give to someone who would be going by sea.

In his usual way, Paul gives some indication of the content of his letter in the address. He addresses it to 'the *ecclesia* of God which is in Corinth'. I have left one word untranslated so that we do not immediately associate it with what the word 'church' means for us. The word *ecclesia* would suggest to a Greek reader a popular assembly, a meeting of citizens called together to make a decision on some important question. To a Jew, it would suggest the people of Israel in the wilderness, particularly as they gathered together to worship God. For Christians the word was given a completely new content: now God had called people together in many places to be a new community with him 'in Christ Jesus'.

That is God's *ecclesia* in this latest period of history. He also has an *ecclesia* in Corinth, but the Christians there should not think that they form the only one.

Paul describes the Corinthian Christians as those who are 'called to be holy'. This rather strange expression has a biblical colouring. In former times, God had redeemed his people from slavery in Egypt to serve him and to live only for him, to be his holy people. 'Holy' means being set apart, called out of the profane world and chosen for the service of God. Anyone who receives such a call, like the Christians, is not yet holy in the moral sense, a holy man. What Paul means is that he will become so in the new community which is focussed on Jesus Christ. It is not a simple matter. To form an *ecclesia* of God in the wilderness, as Israel once did, is much easier than to do the same thing in the middle of a cosmopolitan city.

In his prayer of thanksgiving to God, Paul recounts the many gifts which the Corinthian Christians have received from him. Above all, they have been endowed 'with all words and all knowledge'. But there is still more to come. As he continues with his thanksgiving, Paul refers to the fulfilment that everyone is to expect.

He then goes on to deal one by one with the questions and

the points at issue: everything that he has been told about orally or by letter. He proves to be extremely versatile in doing this. In every question he has to get down to the deepest level, to the essentials, the issue that is really at stake. He likes to think everything through quite radically. That is why we sometimes find him difficult to understand. But at the same time he can be matter-of-fact and practical: 'We do it this way, and that's all there is to it', or: 'Never mind, I will see to the rest when I come.' The reader will also feel how quickly his moods change as he dictates: he can be indignant, sharp, even harsh at times, only to go on to worry that he may have caused offence: or he is tender, happy, ecstatic. The whole letter shows his deep concern.

There might, however, be another reason for his change of mood which we ought to consider further before we go on. As I said earlier, Paul followed his usual practice and dictated this long letter. We can see as much from the way in which he brings it to an end: 'This greeting is in my own hand — PAUL.' It seems unlikely that Paul dictated the whole letter (sixteen chapters in our Bibles!) all at once to one secretary. At least he will have had to stop in order to eat and sleep. He may also have been interrupted by unexpected visitors. What did he do after these interruptions? Did he ask his secretary, 'Where did we get to?' Or, 'Could you just read back that last paragraph (dictated a few moments ago, yesterday, last week)?' We cannot be sure precisely what Paul did, but there were certainly interruptions, and this may explain why he sometimes changes suddenly from one subject or one mood to another.

Some of the intervals in the writing of this letter may have been taken up with conversations between Paul and the Christians from Corinth who were with him. At the end of the letter, he says: 'It is a great pleasure to me that Stephanas, Fortunatus, and Achaicus have arrived . . . they have relieved my mind.' Perhaps these were the ones who brought the letter from Corinth which asked all the questions. Be this as it may, while he was dictating, Paul may well have had more news from Corinth, and he may have been able to discuss the form of his answers with those who brought it.

There is another point which I ought to raise. At an earlier stage I mentioned the possibility that Paul may have made a rough copy of his letters before he began to dictate them; some passages are well thought out, and quite elaborate in form and content. These lead experts in Greek literature to regard Paul as one of the greatest authors of his time. I used to find it hard to believe that while he was dictating, passages of this kind simply came pouring out without any preparation. Now, however, I am not so sure. In fact, they had been years in the making. Paul was constantly pondering every aspect of God's salvation, trying to find the right symbols and terms for it; it was almost as though he was talking to himself. He will also have used the same language when talking to others. So I can understand how, when he was carried away, he may have begun to talk poetically, as though he were reciting a poem, or a hymn, or a confession of faith. Talk like this will have stayed with him; he will not have had to write it down in order to remember it.

Did the people of Paul's time have a better memory than we do? Perhaps they did not need to make notes. Or it may be that at any time a person may be so moved by an event, so impressed by it, that whenever he talks about it he seems to be using well thought out words or even 'literary' forms. At times Paul reminds me of his great predecessor, the prophet Jeremiah. In chapter 36 of the book named after him, we hear how Jeremiah dictated to the scribe Baruch preaching which had been delivered over the course of a great many years. He was forbidden to enter the Temple, so he had to make use of a new medium, the written word, if he was to communicate with the people. In the end, the scroll was also read out to king Jehoiakim, who was sitting by the fire. With perplexing cynicism, the king kept cutting off the columns of the scroll as they were read and throwing them into the fire. Jeremiah thereupon simply asked for another scroll and dictated his words to Baruch all over again. We might regard this as a prodigious feat of memory, but the story does not emphasize it in any way. It is taken for granted that Jeremiah can repeat his earlier preaching, delivered over a period of almost twenty years. In the same way, it seems to me to be quite possible that Paul had certain 'prophetic' sayings so fixed in his mind that he voiced them almost without thinking.

As we read this letter, we shall often come up against one particular difficulty. The Corinthians only needed a hint from Paul to understand what he meant, whereas we are left with a series of question marks. However, we can see the main lines of Paul's approach clearly enough to understand how he deals with the ten questions which the community in Corinth has raised because of its particular situation. As he does so, he gives us a great deal to think about in connection with our own church life. I shall try to comment briefly on each of the ten questions so that his letter is easier to understand.

What Paul seems to find most difficult to take is that there is a threat of divisions (*schismata*) in the community. Some Corinthians said, 'I am for Paul'; others, 'I would choose Apollos'; and yet others, 'My man is Cephas'. There were also those who said, 'I am for Christ', but Paul does not say anything more about this party. The problem evidently centred on three preachers, and on the question which of them was the best. Which of them should one follow to be a good Christian?

Paul reacts violently to this. You seem to have missed the point, he says as he dictates. God has called you out of the world of 'the flesh' to live together 'in Christ', in the power of the Spirit, that is, in a loving community. To achieve this, God makes use of people: of me, of Apollos and of Cephas. If you are going to quarrel over people, argue about who does things best, who has the greatest claim, who is your favourite speaker, then you are heading back to the 'fleshly' world from which you have just been delivered! To start quarrelling, to keep wanting to know better than each other and to be one up on each other is the way of that world.

God has completely different methods. To free us from a sinful and hopeless state of 'the flesh' he chose a completely unexpected and unheard-of approach. He involved himself in a crucifixion, the most horrific way of dying that we know. He acted in a radically different way from what might have been expected by the greatest philosophers and religious geniuses, Greeks and Jews. They had always looked for a super something: only a super-philosopher, a super-power, a super-politician, or (as they kept saying to one another) a super-David could have a chance of 'redeeming' mankind, of achieving a society which had some hope for the future. In his eternal wisdom God had preferred the foolishness of the cross. As a result of this, his creative power, his spirit, broke through, and wherever it was at work it put an end to the works of 'the flesh'. People were made aware of the strange wisdom of God wherever they were touched by the Spirit. And in the context of God's foolish wisdom you could only talk meaningfully with other people who had also come into contact with this Spirit, with 'spiritual' people.

So much for this attempt to describe the beginning of Paul's argument in my own words. You would do better to read and re-read the original. But if you do that you will come up against some obscurities. For we cannot know precisely what differences the Corinthians saw between Paul, Apollos and Cephas.

Moreover, it is often difficult to see what meaning Paul attached to certain terms which he used frequently. Take the term 'word'. When he says that on his first arrival at Corinth he did not testify to God 'in lofty words or wisdom', translators sometimes render the first term as 'eloquence'. But in that case we might ask: was Paul not aware that he was really very eloquent, even in dictating this passage?

Christians, including Paul himself, often used the term 'word' with the meaning 'instruction', 'doctrine'. I have some sympathy with the suggestion that Paul could not compete with Apollos and Cephas when it came to interpretation: knowing the sayings of Jesus and embellishing them in the style of Jewish 'wisdom teachers'. This was the sort of thing that scribes did with the words and precepts of Moses. Perhaps Paul just did not want to compete with them. Perhaps he thought that such an approach amounted to putting something completely new, the power of the spirit, back into the old patterns. In other words, you cannot put new wine into old skins. The result of the kind of teaching favoured by Apollos and Cephas was the formation of a new body of rules, a Christian law. Then people might feel justified in thinking: 'Look, I am doing everything that is required of me, I am not aware of having done any wrong, I am a good Christian; he is not . . .' That might also explain why Paul so rarely talks about Jesus' life and teachings.

Be this as it may, Paul had made a complete and radical break with this form of religion. At the same time, though, he had retained one thing from his past life: his pride. Now, however, this pride was in his weakness, in what God had achieved by means of his weakness.

Another remarkable thing strikes me. When Paul is explaining what part people play in God's plan for the Corinthians, he only talks about himself and Apollos, and never about Peter. Does he want to keep off the subject of Peter? Had Peter not yet been to Corinth? Paul says quite explicitly that Christ is the foundation of the community. Does he mean by this that the foundation is not Cephas, the rock?

Although many question-marks remain, the whole passage (chapters 1–4) remains a powerful piece of writing. By that I mean that it is great, profound, well-expressed and impressive. By 'powerful' I do not mean that it has effective power. For this particular passage has caused divisions (*schismata*) down the ages, and continues to do so: 'I am for Lefebvre; my man is Küng; I stick to Michael Green; I prefer Mascall.' And so on. Perhaps it is impossible to be the *ecclesia* of God as Paul envisaged it.

Some Corinthians had said that Paul would not be coming back to Corinth; indeed, they had begun to boast that he would not dare to reappear. Perhaps this is why Paul now goes on to deal with three points (in chapters 5 and 6) over which the Corinthians might not be quite so self-satisfied. He begins with the case of the man who lives with his stepmother. He wants the Christians to hold as it were a formal assembly and expel the guilty party (the Latin here is 'excommunicate'). In this way, Paul says, the man will be delivered 'to Satan for the destruction of the flesh, so that the spirit may be saved in the day of the Lord'.

What does Paul mean here? When we looked at this letter to the Galatians, we saw that he does not use the terms 'flesh' and 'spirit' to refer to the lower and higher instincts in man. By 'flesh', he means human life, corporate life, which is not transformed or liberated by God's Spirit. This means that human existence is still alienated, sinful, dominated by Satan and doomed to corruption and death. I suspect that such a view underlies Paul's instructions about the judgment which has to be delivered. By persevering in his immoral conduct, this particular man seems to want to remain in the world of the flesh. The community is now to give a solemn endorsement of the choice he has made. In other words, it is to make a solemn pronouncement that the man is to be delivered over to the destructive powers which he himself seems to have preferred.

Since the word 'spirit' which is mentioned here cannot refer to the higher instincts in the man, it can only be a reference to the Christian community. The community is where the Spirit dwells and works, and Paul has already said that the community will have to be holy and blameless on the day when the Lord appears. This point is taken up in the simile which now follows: just as a little yeast permeates a whole lump of dough, so a Christian living a fleshly life can affect an entire community living 'in the Spirit'. We saw in the letter to the Galatians how Paul used a Jewish proverb: 'A little leaven leavens all the dough.' This was a common metaphor for the contagious power of evil. It derived from an ancient custom practised at the Passover. All the old leaven was thrown away and the festival was celebrated by eating new, unleavened bread. Jesus will certainly have stirred his hearers when he compared the power of the kingdom of God with the tiny bit of yeast which a housewife mixes with a large lump of dough. This was his way of expressing his belief that God's saving power was stronger than the corrupt forces of evil.

It must have been very difficult for a community of saints to take shape in the depraved atmosphere of a cosmopolitan port. Paul had already discussed the problems with the Corinthians. What were they to do? Were they to leave Corinth behind and live by the Dead Sea, or on Mount Athos? Certainly not! They were to continue living and working where they were, and to keep up all their old contacts; at the same time, they were to keep the group as pure as possible and avoid any members who might be judged to be fleshly.

The word 'judgment' brings Paul on to another matter of which the self-satisfied Corinthians ought to be ashamed. He has heard that Christians at odds with one another have been taking their disputes to the public courts. In his indignation, he stresses some Jewish teaching which also seems to have been taken over by Christians as they handed on their faith. We have already seen the way in which Jews living in the second century BC expected an end to the world. This is particularly clear in the book of Daniel, the seventh chapter of which has a symbolic account of the destruction of the evil powers of this world by God, who bestows the rule over the world on one 'like a Son of man'. According to the explanation given to Daniel, this figure is a symbol for the 'saints of the Most High'. It represents those Jews who remain faithful to their God despite every kind of persecution, and even in the face of death; because of their steadfastness they will be raised from the dead and be given a share in the coming kingdom of God. As we read Daniel, we must remember that in biblical terminology to rule and to judge are almost synonymous. Jesus, too, was familiar with this identification, as we can see from his promise to the twelve disciples: at the end of the age they are to sit on thrones, judging the twelve tribes of Israel.

When the Corinthians were first instructed in their new faith and were told what was in store for them, they will certainly have been told about the judgment to come. And when they were told about angels, these will not have been the kindly spirits familiar to us from our catechisms, but the invisible powers and forces at work behind nations and law courts, exerting their influence on the world. This, too, was a Jewish idea. The Corinthians, Paul argues, rightly believe that before long they will be judging the world. Yet they ask this very world to pass judgment on their own quarrels. That is stupid. In any case, they should not be quarrelling at all. If they think that they have suffered injury from another brother or have been robbed, why do they stand up for their rights? Why do they have to go to law? 'Why not rather suffer injury?' In the Sermon on the Mount, Jesus taught that his followers were not to resist evil. It is remarkable that Paul does not quote Jesus' words at this point. Can it be that he did not know them?

Paul makes it clear that some of the Corinthians have been

very wicked. However, as he points out in ecstatic mood, 'You have been through the purifying waters; you have been dedicated to God and justified through the name of the Lord Jesus and the Spirit of our God.' That sounds splendid, but unfortunately the reality is rather different. Some Christians in Corinth resort to prostitutes. This is the third point about which they should be ashamed. Yet some of them are proud even of that. Sexual intercourse, they argue, is just as much a natural function as eating and drinking, and since the Spirit of the Lord brings freedom, in this sphere of conduct there are no longer any rules.

Paul disagrees. Sexual intercourse is a different matter from eating and drinking. Eating and drinking do not affect anyone else (though there are instances when this might be the case – Paul will return to them later); sexual intercourse does. In fact the prostitutes in Corinth were employed by the temples, and therefore were involved in idolatry. If, as scripture says, sexual intercourse makes two people one flesh, then consorting with prostitutes unites a Christian with this world, and that is improper. Christians can only be united with their Lord, and the two different relationships are mutually exclusive.

This is a remarkable argument. Paul could have condemned dealings with prostitutes by referring to laws or ethical codes. He could have referred to the moral dangers which are always present when men give way to their desires in this way. For Paul, however, man's physical nature also includes his relationship with others. This is what makes him a man. And because of this Christ, too, has to have a physical resurrection body; otherwise he cannot be Christ for us and we cannot be (the members of) his 'body'. Unlike other sins, consorting with prostitutes (who are also involved in idolatry) is a sin against Christ's body.

'It is a good thing for a man to have nothing to do with women.' Here Paul begins to reply to the questions put to him by the Corinthians in the letter which they sent to Ephesus (chapter 7). Quotation marks were unknown in Paul's day, but it is clear that at this point he is quoting from the letter from Corinth. The completely new way of living experienced by various Christians raised questions for married couples. Some of them seem to have felt inclined to give up sexual intercourse, because they thought that it was inappropriate to their new life in the Spirit. If only the husband or the wife felt this way, then the other partner would feel resentful and might go elsewhere for pleasure or satisfaction.

Paul's answer is clear and decisive. 'The husband must give the wife what is due to her, and the wife equally must give the husband his due.' Both have equal rights and equal duties. They may both refrain from sexual intercourse for spiritual reasons, for example in order to devote themselves more to prayer. But if that is to happen, says Paul, two conditions must be fulfilled. *Both* must be of a common mind, and the period of abstinence should not last too long. Paul is evidently well aware how devout couples can have strong desires as well as noble resolutions.

Paul himself leads a celibate life, but he does so by virtue of a gift which is not bestowed on everyone. It is a good thing for people who are unmarried or no longer married (including widows, though these are a special group which he will discuss shortly) to live like this, at any rate as far as they can.

Paul now goes on to discuss marriage difficulties. He begins with marriages in which both husband and wife are Christians. In such instances there is to be no divorce. This was one of the points on which Jesus clearly went against the Torah. The Torah allowed divorce, or rather, it allowed a husband to put away his wife. The wife had no rights at all. To make her position clear, the Torah required that her husband should provide a bill of divorce. Jesus was a radical champion of the wife's rights. Although putting a wife away was legally permissible for any Jew, Jesus condemned it as a great evil, a fact of which Paul was, of course, aware. However, since in Palestine the wife had no rights, the dispensation given by the Torah only applied to the husband. In Greece, things were different, and it was possible for a wife to divorce her husband.

Paul writes, 'To the married I give this ruling, which is not mine but the Lord's: a wife must not separate herself from her husband; if she does, she must either remain unmarried or be reconciled to her husband; and the husband must not divorce his wife.' It follows from this that if the husband is estranged from his wife he cannot enter into another marriage, though Paul does not say so in as many words. It is significant that he begins with the wife, and the possibility that she may take the first steps towards a divorce. One would hardly expect this from a Jew. Is there a reflection of Paul's own experience here?

Be this as it may, Paul now considers another possibility, when only one of the couple is a Christian. In itself, this is no reason for divorce. It cannot be argued that one of them is involved in a completely new set of relationships, in Christ, in the Spirit, whereas the other partner, the non-believer, is still completely caught up in the world of the flesh. The situation here is different from that of casual intercourse with a pagan prostitute: the lasting relationship brings the unbeliever into the new situation and 'sanctifies' him or her, together with their children.

There may, however, be tensions which make it impossible for a couple to live together. In that case, if the heathen partner wants a separation, he or she may have it. The marriage bond can be broken. Unfortunately, the secretary to whom Paul was dictating could not reproduce Paul's mood when he said, 'God's call is a call to live in peace . . . . Think of it: as a wife you may be your husband's salvation; as a husband you may be your wife's salvation.' Perhaps there was a touch of sadness in Paul's voice: he himself had not been so lucky. . .

The enthusiastic Corinthians evidently tended to express their new experiences in ways which Paul thought unnecessary. Here, too, he is apprehensive about excessive or misguided enthusiasm. If one partner in a marriage becomes a Christian and the other does not, and there is no prospect of peace, it is better for them to part company. Otherwise each one is to remain in the state of life in which he or she was on becoming a believer. Paul takes circumcision as his first example: 'Circumcision or uncircumcision is neither here nor there; what matters is to keep God's commands.' This might seem an odd remark for Paul to make, but it was certainly not intended in the Jewish sense (the commandment to be circumcised was one of the most important in the Torah). By 'God's commands', Paul understood everything required of those who became believers and attached themselves to Christ.

Paul's second example is that of the slave. Slaves are not to resent their status. If they can obtain their freedom, well and good; as free men, they can become the Lord's slaves. All Christians have been bought by Christ and now belong wholly to him.

As his third example Paul now takes a group of people whom he calls *parthenoi*. These are probably men and women who are not yet married. I have some sympathy with the view that here he is thinking particularly of engaged couples, those who are in some way committed to each other. One such couple in Corinth may well have asked, 'Should we go ahead and get married?'

'You certainly may,' says Paul, 'but I would not advise it.' The Lord will appear very soon, and Paul feels that it would be better for Christians to remember that and to prepare for his coming. 'What I mean, my friends, is this. The time we live in will not last long. While it lasts, married men should be as if they had no wives; mourners should be as if they had nothing to grieve them, the joyful as if they did not rejoice; buyers must not count on keeping what they buy, nor those who use the world's wealth on using it to the full. For the whole frame of this world is passing away.'

Those who marry and are concerned that their marriage should work out well cannot devote themselves to the Lord's work as whole-heartedly as those who remain single. The Lord, who is coming soon, will then bring together all his followers in one community. At the same time, however, Paul recognizes that it is very difficult for a young man who is deeply in love to refrain permanently from expressing his love towards his betrothed. In that case, he says, there is no harm in marrying. You should only refrain from marriage if you feel that this is something that you can do. 'He who marries his partner does well, and he who does not will do better.'

Would Paul have torn up this chapter, had he known that it was going to be regarded as holy scripture? No, indeed had he known he would never have written in this way. His whole approach to the subject, and what we so often regard as his underestimation of marriage, is governed by his belief that there will be no future even for holy scriptures: the Lord himself will soon appear. Readers in later centuries often forgot this.

117

Of course, Paul knew nothing of the positive estimation of human sexuality which has developed since in our culture. We cannot blame him for thinking only of the husband, or in the case of the engaged couple for talking only about the desires of the young man and not about those of his fiancée. Still less, given his Jewish background, does it occur to him that a relationship between two people of the same sex might be felt to be God-given.

Paul uses this last term to describe his own celibate condition. He is able to live like this, he writes, by virtue of a charisma, a gift of the Spirit which is not bestowed on everyone. He is realistic enough to accept this fact, though in view of the imminent coming of the Lord, he would wish that things were otherwise.

It is striking that despite all the talk of marriage and divorce and celibacy, Paul never uses the word 'love' once! He does, however, use it as soon as he goes on to the question of meat offered to idols. This is another point on which the Corinthians differed and about which they had asked Paul for his opinion (chapter 8).

Some Corinthians evidently argued like this. 'We all know by faith that there is only one God. Other gods are idols and do not exist. Meat offered to them is therefore just ordinary meat and so eating it cannot have any effect on our relationship with the one God.' So on this level too, anything was possible. Paul shares this belief, but goes on to say that other Christians have not got so far. And as long as some Christians have difficulties about eating meat offered to idols, it is wrong to act in this way without further thought. What matters here is not the knowledge of faith, but one's fellow Christians.

All this is said in the terse but meaningful remarks with which Paul begins. The Corinthians say, 'We all have knowledge.' Paul retorts, ' "Knowledge" puffs up, but love builds up. If any imagines that he knows something, he does not yet know as he ought to know. But if one loves God, one is known (by him).'

One might almost say that there is a contrast here between Paul's biblical way of thinking and the Greek approach adopted by the Corinthians. Brought up on the Old Testament, when Paul hears the phrase 'know someone' he thinks of affection, love and fellowship. When the Old Testament says that God 'knows' men it means that he loves them, enters into relationship with them and brings them into communion with him. Whenever someone comes to believe and receives the Spirit, the Bible says that he is known by God. Thus in Paul's letter to the Galatians we read, 'Formerly, when you did not know God, you were in bondage to beings that by nature are no gods; but now that you have come to know God, or rather to be known by God . . .'

When Paul listens to the Corinthians talking about knowing, there does not seem to be any reference to relationships. They seem to be thinking in terms of theoretical knowledge, objective insight. And when they say that this kind of knowledge is a gift which has been given them, they become proud and boastful and think themselves a cut above their foolish fellow-Christians who have not got so far, and whom they have offended by their free and easy way of eating meat offered to idols. They are not to go on like this, Paul says, because true knowledge consists in the recognition that the important thing is the salvation of one's fellow-Christians, for whom Christ died.

Paul calls this attitude towards others 'love', *agape*. Later on in the letter he describes love at much greater length. Here he says that love dwells in a man when he is loved by God. According to the oldest copy of the letter that we have, Paul dictated the words I mentioned above but without the two mentions of God, which were therefore added later. In other words, he said, 'If a man loves (his fellow man), he is known (by God).'

When men are moved (known, loved, called) by God in this way, their love for one another leads them to form a community, which Paul often describes as a building, a house or home. Consequently, when he is talking about love he is fond of speaking of building up, edifying. He does this above all in this particular letter to a group in which Christians who have a high opinion of themselves and think themselves to be wise are making all the running.

Paul ends his plea for the 'weak' Christians with a passage in which, quite strikingly, he goes over into the first person: 'In thus sinning against your brothers and wounding their conscience, you sin against Christ. And therefore, if food be the downfall of my brother, I will never eat meat any more, for I will not be the cause of my brother's downfall.'

He then goes on (in chapter 9) to ask some agitated questions about himself. 'Am I not a free man? Am I not an apostle? Did I not see Jesus our Lord? Are you not my own handiwork, in the Lord?' People have obviously been criticizing him, and so he throws questions back at them: 'Have I no right to eat and drink? Have I no right to take a Christian wife about with me, like the rest of the apostles and the Lord's brothers, and Cephas? Or are Barnabas and I alone bound to work for our living?'

I suspect that this is one of those points where Paul was interrupted while dictating. Perhaps he had been talking in the meantime with someone from Corinth, Stephanas, for example, who had told him about criticisms which were going the rounds in Corinth. The apostles from Jerusalem had given instructions about meat offered to idols, and these were very clear. Why, then, was Paul proving so difficult? He couldn't really be a true apostle. He had no commission from Jesus himself. That was clear from the way in which he behaved. For example, unlike the real apostles, he did not want other Christians to support him, although this was something that Jesus himself had commanded. The real apostles also expected provision to be made for their wives, whom they took with them on their travels. Paul did not do this (at any rate he did not do this any more), and he was proud that he did not accept any money from those whom he had converted.

As we read Paul's self-defence we are not only amazed at his devotion but also somewhat repelled by the way in which he puts forward his own behaviour as a model. I am struck first of all by his experience of a relationship with Christ which is extraordinarily profound and is bound up with his unique vocation to represent (in the most literal sense of the word) the force of Christ's love in the final and most decisive period of history.

Moreover, here he is speaking to Christians who have a very high opinion of themselves, whereas in fact they really have no understanding of the most important thing of all, love, that is, concern and care for the well-being of others. And this is precisely what characterizes Paul as Christ's representative. These Christians also think that now they have been initiated through baptism and the eucharist, and are richly endowed with knowledge and ecstasy, they are already in possession of eternal salvation. Paul, however, tells them that even he is uncertain of salvation, despite his utter dedication to the salvation of others.

This is why (in chapter 10) he presents a kind of sermon based on the story of what happened to the Israelites in the wilderness. They were guided by God himself, yet many of them came to grief. We might suppose that at this point Paul is recalling a sermon which he had preached some time before, biblical texts and all. After it, he returns to the question of meat offered to idols and ends with an appeal to the Corinthians to follow him in his care and devotion towards others, just as he follows Christ.

The next three points are concerned with what happens when the Corinthians meet for worship. Apparently Paul's visitors from Corinth had talked to him about the first two (chapter 11). The important thing for us is his starting point: he and those to whom he writes seem to be agreed on it. The spirit came upon women as well as men; women, too, could suddenly fall into ecstasy and 'speak in tongues' or 'prophesy'. When that happened, some Corinthians thought the women should take off the veils they usually wore. Others differed and arguments arose. Paul produces a series of profound arguments which are clearly inspired by themes of Jewish theology. He also supposes that angels, too, are present when the Christians meet for worship: perhaps he imagines them as guardians of God's creation. He also seems to be saying that in the new situation, now that the Spirit has come, the veil is no longer a sign of subordination; it is a token of an authority which now has also been given to women. Still, he also sees that his arguments may seem somewhat dubious, so in the end he simply states that it is important to observe the custom which has become established not only in Corinth, but in other Christian communities. Here, too, the Corinthians must not introduce innovations simply because they have the Spirit.

The second point concerns the way in which Christians meet together for a common meal. The way things are, this is anything but 'the Lord's supper'. The differences between the rich and the poor members of the *ecclesia* are painfully evident. The food contributed by those who come is not shared out fairly. The rich arrive with their delicacies and are already full by the time that the workers, after their long hours, eventually appear. It is not easy for people from such different backgrounds and with habits which are so deeply ingrained to join together as brothers and sisters in a common meal. It would be better for them to have their meals at home in the usual way, the rich among the rich and the poor among the poor.

What they can and must do together, however, is to share in the simple food which the Lord provides, the bread and the wine in which he gives himself as the sacrifice of the new covenant. These actions express the ultimate unity of all men: for the moment it is to be seen only as a mysterious reality which will not fully be revealed until the end of all things. At that time the Lord who endured death for all men will return as their judge. Paul seems to see this future judgment already at work among members of the community who are smitten by illness and death: they have failed to recognize the real character of the bread and the wine, and have not understood them as tokens of sharing in the body and blood of Christ.

The third and last point was raised by the Corinthians in the letter which they sent to Paul: they want to know how to deal with the abundance of gifts sent by the Spirit (chapters 12–14). Paul begins by pointing out in a matter-of-fact kind of way that the Corinthians are already familiar with the ecstatic experiences of which they are so proud from their pagan past. Now, however, here too Jesus has become the only Lord. He is the sole source from which all the workings of the Spirit stem. Paul sums them up and deliberately puts the highly prized speaking with tongues in last place. Although he, too, had received this gift, Paul spends some time making it clear that 'prophecy' is much more important. The community is much more in need of people who can talk impressively about the faith in a way that others can understand. The good of the whole community is always paramount, and the community will benefit if its members can understand what is being said. In his long discussion (chapter 14), Paul uses the words 'building' and 'build up' over and over again. It is as though when he was reading through this passage he remembered what he had said earlier in the letter: 'building up' is possible only through love. It was perhaps after this that he wrote the famous chapter about love (chapter 13, which seems to be an insertion between chapters 12 and 14); he may well have worked out parts of it beforehand.

Nevertheless, this chapter too is addressed directly to the Corinthians. It is sometimes called Paul's hymn of love, but if we put ourselves in the Corinthians' shoes we can see what a disconcerting effect it must have had. Paul tells them that all the things of which they are so proud do not matter in God's eyes. They believe that speaking with tongues is the most important sign of God's presence with them; but speaking with tongues, being able to prophesy so that others can understand, and having profound knowledge, are no more indications of virtuosity in religious affairs. The Corinthians may give away all their belongings and be so dedicated that they burn themselves, an Indian practice which will have been known about in Greece. Nevertheless, these striking acts of unselfishness and heroism can be motivated by a desire for publicity, for fame, a concern to surpass others in religious devotion. And that means that those involved with such actions are worthless and even wicked; in any case, they are alienated from God. With him, the only thing that matters is love.

'Love is patient and kind; love is not jealous or boastful; it is not arrogant or rude. Love does not insist on its own way; it is not irritable or resentful; it does not rejoice at wrong, but rejoices in the right. Love bears all things, believes all things, hopes all things, endures all things.'

Some of the Corinthians who heard this read out may well have begun to wonder, 'Does Paul really mean that? Is it really true that all these other powerful expressions of religious belief count for nothing if people do not act towards one another in this way in their daily life?' As they went on listening, they will have realized that this was what Paul really did mean. What he says may sound ordinary, but what he is asking for is limitless love, love which embraces the whole of life. That is clear from the way in which 'all things' is repeated four times in the last sentence.

Those who love, support others in their need and share in the burden of their weakness: as the last clause puts it, they 'endure' all the pain that others cause. Faith and hope for one's fellow-men go with an attitude of trust in *all* circumstances, a belief that the other person and his welfare is the most important thing of all.

After his description of the way in which love is expressed, Paul turns to the workings of the Spirit which the Corinthians have experienced. This time it is not to point out how useless they are without love, but to show that unlike love they are only transitory. They are aspects of the Corinthians' present situation. True, the Corinthians have received the Spirit, but this is merely a pledge, an advance payment on the full amount which will be handed over later. It is worth noting that Paul mentions the three most valued gifts of the Spirit first, prophecy, speaking with tongues and knowledge, and then says nothing more about speaking with tongues. Perhaps he does this deliberately in view of what he is going to say next: all these gifts vanish when the perfect comes. At this point he goes over into the first person. I am a Christian, he argues, with an exceptionally deep insight into the mystery of God's salvation. I have much greater spiritual gifts than any Corinthian. But I know that anything I say is childish chatter and anything I feel or think is puerile compared with the perfection that I shall attain when I stand before God face to face. And to come into the presence of God is the destiny of all men.

'Love never ends; as for prophecies, they will pass away; as for tongues, they will cease; as for knowledge, it will pass away. For our knowledge is imperfect and our prophecy is imperfect; but when the perfect comes, the imperfect will pass away. When I was a child, I spoke like a child, I thought like a child, I reasoned like a child; when I became a man, I gave up childish ways. For now we see in a mirror dimly, but then face to face. Now I know in part; then I shall understand fully, even as I have been fully understood.'

Paul ends this profound chapter with a sentence which can still surprise us. He has been contrasting daily expressions of love with the extraordinary manifestations of the Spirit. Now all at once he brings in faith and hope, which have not been part of his discussion at all so far. 'So faith, hope, love abide, these three; but the greatest of these is love.'

In his first letter, to the Christians in Thessalonica, Paul had already spoken of their faith in God, their hope for the coming of Christ and their love for one another. Perhaps it was already usual for Christians of the time to sum up the basic features of their new life-style under these three words. In that case the Corinthians too will already have been familiar with the three-some faith, hope and love. Perhaps Paul added this surprising conclusion because he could hear the Corinthians saying to themselves, 'Yes, but there are faith and hope as well as love.' 'Agreed,' says Paul, 'there are certainly "these three". But the greatest of them is love.' And there he stops. Now is not the time for him to point out that faith and hope are also among the transient features of Christian life. They too will disappear when we find our fulfilment in God.

Let me add two comments which may help when you think about this chapter. First, it is quite remarkable that Paul makes no mention here of the person of Jesus. But this hymn to love could never have been written had Jesus not shown in his life how closely religion, the service of God, was bound up with the service of one's fellow man. Certainly Jesus is not mentioned here, but we might say that this was unnecessary; in the last resort, it is Jesus himself who speaks here through Paul in language determined by the circumstances of the Corinthians.

What Jesus began was new, so new that Christians chose an unusual Greek word with which to describe it, *agape*. The Greeks had all kinds of words to express the emotions that people feel for one another. One of them was *eros*, which lies behind our word 'erotic'. The Greek translators of the Jewish Bible had used the word *agape* and the corresponding verb in passages which spoke of God's love for his people and of the love which the Israelites ought to have for God. Now, however, the Christians filled the word with new content which had been given to it by Jesus and his unselfish and utter dedication.

We do not have any special word for Christian love in our language. For us love can simply mean being attracted by; it can have merely erotic connotations. But it can also be used in a Christian sense. The good Samaritan in Jesus' story was certainly not attracted by the wounded Jew lying at the side of the road. But according to Jesus, he 'loved' him. He was moved by compassion, moved to offer the help that he himself would have wanted had he been in the same position.

When I join others in listening to Paul's description of *agape*, I am often asked: 'Don't I have to "feel" for someone if I am to love him or her in a Christian way?' I usually reply by asking another question. As a person grows in faith, may he or she not come to see others, who may be unattractive or hostile, as fellow human beings, as partners in the mystery of human existence which God alone can bring to its conclusion, and may he or she not come to feel for others on this deeper level? In this connection I like to think of the deep love of a husband and wife for each other. It begins with mutual attraction, with. *eros*, but over the course of years it turns into *agape*. All the threats posed by a merely erotic relationship (possessiveness, jealousy, lack of trust) lose their force. Their love has become so deep that they can extend it to others.

Where we tend to speak of a 'deep' love, of love on a 'deeper level' which can be shown towards someone who is unattractive, Paul, who is not as restrained as we are, uses the words 'God' and 'Spirit'; he mentions the name of Christ, who died for others. For Paul, it is God who awakens *agape* in a man. But the remarkable thing is that this love is always directed towards other human beings, and never towards God. Paul was a Jew, and will have often heard the summons, 'Hear, O Israel, you shall love God with all your heart.' It is only rarely that he calls the believers 'those who love God'. But whenever he is talking explicitly about man's attitude towards the God who loves him, he speaks of faith, trust, surrender, obedience, and never of love. Paul has evidently been so moved by Christ that he sees the *agape* aroused in men by the Spirit only as directed to their fellow human beings.

I just want to add a comment about a few sentences at the end of chapter 14. There we read: 'As in all congregations of God's people, women should not address the meeting. They have no licence to speak, but should keep their place as the law directs. If there is something they want to know, they can ask their own husbands at home. It is a shocking thing that a woman should address the congregation.'

Some distinguished scholars who are very familiar with Paul's work think that this passage was inserted into the letter by a later hand. They argue that the vocabulary and above all the tone and style of this paragraph are closer to the later, and very different, letters to Timothy and Titus than to Paul himself. Moreover, the paragraph interrupts Paul's argument. Above all, however, it does not agree with what Paul says with approval earlier on in the letter, namely that women are as free as men to pray and even prophesy when the community meets. No argument can be conclusive, but I think that these objections have much to commend them. Paul is by no means consistent, and he can certainly change his tactics depending on circumstances. There were good reasons why he had to keep protesting that he was honest and consistent. He would never have done this had people not made accusations against him. But that women should play their part in Christian worship seems to me to be an integral part of Paul's vision, his insight into the faith. 'In Christ', distinctions and differences no longer matter, even if they are the differences between men and women.

However, we must leave Paul's discussion of such problems and come on to his most important point, the question of the resurrection of the dead. Paul deliberately ends with it. All the previous points were to do with belief and its consequences, and with love as the beginning of a shared life 'in Christ'. But this shared life is shot through with expectation, with the hope of fulfilment.

The Corinthians had some difficulty with the way in which this was described as a physical resurrection from the dead. Their ideas had been shaped by the culture of ancient Greece. The Greeks were obsessed with the idea that the physical aspect of the world, matter, was bad. They saw it as a kind of divine by-product, waste from the spiritual activity of creation. Every man had a spiritual element in him, but the body got in the way of it. Men could be happy only when this spiritual nucleus had been released, and that would happen when they were freed from the prison of their bodies. Anyone accustomed to think in this way would hardly think it good news to be told that the redeemer, the saviour, had been restored to bodily life after death, and that he also had power to give his followers their physical bodies back after death. 'Thank you very much,' would have been the reaction, 'but that is precisely what we do *not* want.'

We have already seen that the hope for a resurrection after death arose in the Jewish community. It emerged from the belief that everything had one origin and as the consequence of a kind of unitary vision of man and the world. Man is a whole, made up of both spirit and body; mankind is a whole, one great family with one ancestor; and the universe has been made for the sake of mankind. At the time of the persecution in the second century before Christ people began to expect that because the world had become so corrupt, God would make a new one, and that even the Jews who had died for their faith would have a share in it. They too would be recreated in physical human form. As a Jew, Paul expected this, and his encounter with Christ made him certain that God had now begun on this new creation.

We do not know precisely how the Corinthians had reconciled the message of Christ's resurrection with their Greek way of thinking about man and the world. Perhaps a great many of them were so taken up with their mysterious experience of the Spirit and the wonderful insight it gave them that they felt themselves already to be sharing in the risen life of the Lord, and hardly thought of the fulfilment to come. Paul also mentions that some people had themselves baptized on behalf of others, probably relatives, who had died without having a chance to be baptized and thus to be united with Christ. So they believed that the dead were still within reach and continued to exist in some way.

Whatever his Corinthians may have thought and said, Paul simply handed on his message in the words which had been passed down to him; 'that Christ died for our sins, in accordance with the scriptures; that he was buried: and that he appeared to

Cephas, and afterwards to the Twelve.' Paul then goes on to name other people to whom Jesus has appeared; at the end of the list he adds himself, the persecutor, a monster . . .

What he then goes on to say can hardly be called an explanation. He simply remarks that if Christ is not risen, then what we believers say and do is nonsense. If Christ is not risen, we are captives in the world of 'the flesh', dominated by hostile forces and devilish powers around us and within us, subject to sin and death. In that case we have no prospects at all. But Christ is indeed risen, the first representative of a new mankind which will be filled with God's saving power, just as he is. Here Paul again uses the biblical approach that I have called a 'unitary vision': mankind is one because it is descended from one ancestor and summed up in one person: Christ represents the new mankind. Was Paul aware that this way of thinking must have seemed very strange to Greeks?

He now takes up the question how people are to imagine the risen body, giving illustrations from nature. The seed dies in the ground, and what then comes up has quite a different nature.

So it is with the resurrection of the dead. What is sown in the earth as a perishable thing is raised imperishable. Sown in humiliation, it is raised in glory; sown in weakness, it is raised in power.

Increasingly enraptured over what may be expected, Paul finally dares to contemplate the 'mystery', the consummation that is to come. His words remind us of the passage in his letter to Thessalonica which we looked at earlier. However, out of the imagery usually associated with this subject, only the trumpet appears.

The trumpet will sound, and the dead will be raised, imperishable, and we shall be changed as well, because our present perishable nature must put on imperishability and this mortal nature must put on immortality . . . then the words of scripture will come true: *Death is swallowed up in victory.*

Hostile powers like sin, the Law (which makes things even worse for the man who lives 'in the flesh') and death may still be active. But the end is in sight for all of them.

So let us thank God for giving us the victory through our Lord Jesus Christ.

In this rapture Paul has not lost all his common sense. Because the ultimate victory is so sure, the Corinthians must now press on eagerly with 'the work of the Lord', about which he has written in his letter. They are to take care of, and build up, the 'body of Christ', the life of which consists in service and true love. They can be certain that the work they take pains over here will never be wasted.

Chapter 15 raises once again the question posed to us by Paul's letter to Thessalonica. His expectation of an imminent end to the world came to nothing, and we cannot share it. Because our view of the world, the universe, space and time is so different we can no longer think of God 'intervening' in this way.

Our question is: can we still make anything of Paul's expectation? How far can we follow him in looking for final fulfilment for each one of us after death? When it comes to questions like this, I try to keep in mind the origins of Paul's expectations. They are based on a particular form of belief in God. He was steeped in this belief from childhood on; it was his life. He had faith in, and entrusted himself to, a God who keeps faith despite everything, and who can and will make something completely new even out of ashes.

Because it now comes naturally to me to approach everything in a historical way, I shall begin by mentioning the first clear expressions of the belief which Paul inherited. We can see them at the time of the Babylonian captivity. All visible signs of God's 'covenant' with his people had then been removed: Jerusalem and the Temple had been devastated and God's people had been driven out of his land. He seemed to have abandoned them, with some justification, because they had not obeyed his covenant. They had parted company with him, and as a nation they were now dead. Yet even then there were believers who said, 'But God will make a new beginning.'

One of them was Ezekiel. In chapter 37 of his book there is a good expression of this belief. Ezekiel sees a wide valley full of dead bones. 'Here is the people of Israel. They think to themselves, "Our bones are dried up, our hope has fled, it is all up with us." ' Then Ezekiel watches the wind of God, his life-giving Spirit, blowing over the valley: the bones become living people who begin to stand up, 'an innumerable host'.

Over the following centuries this belief in God's faithfulness, his power and his purpose to make a new beginning, leads to the expectation of a 'world to come'. We have already considered the idea before. Jesus shared in this expectation, but he gave it new content. For some time now I have come to see more clearly than before a connection between his 'ministry' (what he said and did) and his disciples' belief that God had 'raised him from the dead'. Let me put it in this way.

Jesus spoke and acted for a God who could not bear isolation. God wanted everyone to belong within his community. Jesus showed what his God so wanted by healing people who had been cut off from others and who felt abandoned by God because they were ill, and their illness was regarded as the work of Satan. He cured the lame, the blind, the dumb, the deaf, the lepers, the possessed. But he also showed God's concern by eating with those who for other religious reasons were thought to be outside God's community: the unclean and the sinners. (Sharing a meal is an important sign of friendship in eastern countries.) His radical opposition to all these forms of isolation cost him his life. But his sole aim was to create real community, of the kind to which he pointed so vividly at the last supper.

Those who had travelled around with him and had seen Jesus' urge to meet people and bring them together, his irresistible dynamism, simply could not believe that God had abandoned him in the utter loneliness of death. So I suppose that Jesus' own belief in God's desire for men to belong together and his attempts to do something about it led his disciples to believe that God had not abandoned Jesus even in death. So by dying, he had come alive in a new way, near to God and in his presence.

A Jew would find it difficult to envisage such a 'life' other than in physical terms. So the disciples took it for granted that Jesus had come out of his tomb. However, it is quite impossible to imagine a physical life with, as Paul puts it somewhere, 'no more death'. In this chapter all he can say is that this is a completely different sort of bodily life from our own, illustrating the point from the different kinds of matter in the universe as he and his Corinthians know it.

Not all New Testament writers follow Paul in thinking and speaking about the resurrection of Jesus as a physical resurrection. Sometimes they simply say that Jesus has been raised or exalted. But they all believe that he died and is now alive. It also seems possible to talk like this without mentioning a physical body. All the New Testament writers are sure that they and their fellow-Christians, whether as individuals or in groups, are in contact with the living Lord and have a living relationship with him. But they all talk about it in different ways. We have already heard Paul telling the Philippians from prison in Ephesus how much Christ means to him and how death would be a positive gain: this would make his relationship with Christ unbreakable and utterly complete.

Perhaps we can now consider the question which was posed by Paul's letter to Thessalonica. He was sure about two things: first, Christ would come quickly, even during the lifetime of his generation; but secondly, the precise time of his coming was unknown. Everyone surely knows of a similar kind of certainty: I know that I shall experience it myself, but I do not know precisely when. That is the way in which we talk about death. Everyone will find that death suddenly steals up on them, but no one knows when; it comes 'like a thief in the night'. We would be taking up Paul's way of thinking in his letter to the Philippians if we were to replace the impersonal, negative word death here by another word, Christ. Christ's coming has the same total and irrevocable character as death, but it is utterly positive. That is why Paul could say: for me death is gain. His relationship with Christ was all-important for his life, but it was not yet complete or definitive.

Perhaps this is a way of sharing the essence of Paul's belief without his expectation that Christ would soon return in the sight of all men, in the cosmic event which he also mentions to his Corinthians.

I have described the specific belief in God from which Jewish expectations for the future emerged and the way in which it was given entirely new content by the Christ event. I am firmly convinced that this kind of belief is the essential feature that unites Christians and forms a link between the generations.

Such a belief cannot be handed on without words, formulas, symbols, ideas. However, these must change with every phase of a culture. Even then, they are meaningless if they are not the expression of an attitude, a way of life, a concern.

⟝ 10 ⟞

Philemon: *Agape* in Action

While he was in prison in Ephesus, Paul was visited by a young man who had committed a serious crime. The man was a slave belonging to a certain Philemon, who lived in or near the city of Colossae, a hundred miles or so inland. The slave had run away from his owner, which meant that in effect he had robbed him. There were heavy penalties for runaway slaves throughout the Roman empire. In Italy there was an organization for tracking down runaway slaves, but perhaps this was not the case in the province of Asia. In any case, if Philemon got his slave back again, he had the right to punish him. We learn from contemporary documents that runaway slaves were flogged and sometimes branded; they might even be crucified.

The man who sought Paul's help was called Onesimus, which was a common name for a slave: it means 'useful' or 'profitable'. Perhaps Onesimus had heard his master talking about this remarkable man Paul, a kind of philosopher, to whom Philemon owed a new approach to life. Be this as it may, instead of disappearing into the great city of Ephesus or seeking work abroad, well out of reach of his master, Onesimus ventured to present himself at the prison. For a wanted criminal, this was like going into the lions' den. And when he got there, he asked to see a friend of his master!

Paul will have given the young man a warm welcome. He must have told Onesimus why he was in prison. It was because of what he called 'the gospel', the message of Jesus the Christ, the very message that he had passed on to Philemon. Onesimus was struck by what Paul said, and resolved to dedicate his life to Christ and become a member of the new community. He wanted to join Paul in his work.

However, as we already know, other people's enthusiasm made Paul very matter-of-fact. Paul might certainly seem less than sympathetic in telling a runaway slave to go back to his master, even at the risk of being punished harshly. I can hear Paul talking to Onesimus rather like this: 'The law says that you belong to Philemon; you are part of his property. You have robbed him by running away. And perhaps you've stolen money from him into the bargain. In any case, you must go back to your master. But don't worry. Philemon, too, has become a Christian. I've told you that Christians treat one another in quite a different way; they form a new kind of community. No one is left to himself; we all help one another. I now belong to you and you belong to me, and we stand up for one another. Both of us belong to Philemon and his community in Colossae. Go back there with an easy mind. You will discover that the presence of Christ among us men is a reality. Of course, there is nothing that I would like better than for you to come to Ephesus and help me in Christ's cause, but by rights you belong to Philemon. It is up to him to give you your freedom. I will give you a letter to take to him.'

We have the letter which Paul sent. This is quite remarkable, when we remember that at least one whole letter to the Corinthians has been lost, and that will have contained much more important matters than this one particular case of Onesimus the slave. Why was it preserved? It has been supposed that the Onesimus who later became a leading figure in the church at Ephesus was none other than the slave whom Paul befriended. In that case he will have kept Paul's letter because it was so important to him. It has also been supposed that he had a hand in collecting Paul's letters together, and added this particular one which concerned himself. However, the real reason for the preservation of this short letter may have been the kind of letter it is. It may be about a 'particular case', but the way in which Paul deals with the case has a lot to say to other readers.

First of all, Paul did not regard this as a particularly private matter. We can see from the address that the letter is not strictly a personal one: Paul is not simply writing to Philemon. Both have links with others in Christ, and all are working together to build up the new community. The letter comes not only from Paul but from his brother Timothy, and it is addressed not only to Philemon but to Apphia 'our sister', who was presumably Philemon's wife. The escape and return of the slave Onesimus would obviously affect her, as the one who ran the household. But she was also involved, by virtue of being a member of the *ecclesia* which met in Philemon's house. Archippus, who is also mentioned, will probably have been another member of the household.

So the letter will have been sent to be read aloud to the Christians who met at Philemon's house. We must remember this when reading the thanksgiving which, as usual, follows the address. Paul thanks God because he has heard of Philemon's love and faith (in that order!). He then expresses the hope that Philemon will come to see the good that can be done 'among us' through faith in Christ, who shapes men's lives in the present and who will come again in the near future. By now Paul has already forgotten what he said in his prayer, and says it to Philemon once again: 'I have derived much joy and comfort from your love, my brother, because the hearts of the saints have been refreshed through you.'

The word translated 'hearts' here literally means 'bowels', that part of the body from which, according to the Bible, men's deepest feelings come. Paul uses the same word when he tells the Corinthians how much Titus cares for them ('God puts the same earnest care for you into the heart of Titus') and also when he tells them how his own heart is wide. The same word appears twice in Paul's letter to his favourite community of Philippi. Paul uses it three more times in this short letter to Philemon.

By virtue of his 'boldness' as an apostle of Christ, Paul has the right to tell Philemon what he ought to do; instead, he prefers to appeal to his love. Philemon is to remember that Paul is an old man (that could mean that he was about fifty), in prison for Christ's sake. Just as the Corinthians had become his 'children' when he brought the gospel to them, so too in prison Onesimus, whom he is now sending back, has become a son. He is 'my very heart'.

Philemon has the right to take back Onesimus as his slave, but at the same time Paul asks him to receive Onesimus as his dear brother in Christ. Paul himself is ready to make good any damage Onesimus may have done his master. However, Philemon is really in Paul's debt. . .

Paul ends his short plea with a play on the name Onesimus: 'Yes, brother, I want some benefit from you in the Lord. Refresh my heart in Christ.'

In the confidence that Philemon will be obedient (to the 'law' of *agape*) and do more than Paul asks, Paul makes one last request: will Philemon make a room ready for him, 'for I am hoping through my prayers to be granted to you.'

We must imagine that this letter was read out aloud to Philemon's household and that Onesimus was there too. What could Philemon do but embrace his slave, give him his freedom, and send him back to help Paul in Ephesus?

— 11 —

Conflict with the Corinthians

In the postscript to his long letter to the Corinthians, Paul described his plans. He meant to remain in Ephesus until Pentecost, after which he would travel through Macedonia to Corinth, where he hoped to spend the winter. Meanwhile the Corinthians would be hard at work collecting money for the Christian community in Jerusalem. Perhaps he would accompany those who were to take the collection there. '

However, things did not turn out as Paul had planned. This emerges from his further correspondence with the Christian community in Corinth. When I say 'correspondence' I mean precisely that, because what in our Bible is called the Second Letter to the Corinthians looks like a collection of several of Paul's letters. From it we can discover that after sending the longer epistle, the 'first' letter, he found himself in violent conflict with his Corinthian Christians. The 'second letter' is our only source of information about the argument, and we have to use guesswork to discover why it arose, how it turned out and who was involved. Nothing can be inferred from Acts. Those to whom Paul wrote will have known more about the details than we can. All I can do here is to suggest what may have happened. My reconstruction needs to have a great many question-marks put against it, but at least it may provide a background against which to read the Second Letter to the Corinthians. If we can understand it more clearly, our picture of Paul will be that much less blurred.

As I have just said, Paul had wanted to go to Corinth via Philippi and Thessalonica (Macedonia) in order to spend the winter there. For some reason, he went earlier than planned.

He sailed straight there and intended to use Corinth as a base from which to visit Macedonia. That meant two visits to Corinth instead of one.

Perhaps he went straight to Corinth because he was worried. Had he heard that the moral conduct of the Christians there left a great deal to be desired? Or had he had news of more intruders? In either event, his visit was a bitter disappointment.

'Apostles' had in fact come to Corinth with quite different ideas from Paul. They could boast of pure Jewish descent (Paul mentions honorary titles such as Hebrews, Israelites, the seed of Abraham). They brought credentials with them, perhaps from people who had been personally called by Jesus. These letters qualified them as true 'servants of Christ'. Their ecstatic gifts provided further confirmation of this.

The missionaries were certainly different from those who had come to Galatia. Paul does not accuse them of wanting to impose circumcision and the Law on the Corinthian Christians. Nor is there any clear indication that they wanted to put into effect the four regulations mentioned in Luke's account of the meeting in Jerusalem: to refrain from 'unchastity', from meat offered to gods, from meat containing blood in it and from blood. Did they have anything to do with the Cephas party? Were their credentials signed by the leaders in Jerusalem? Did they make their mark in Corinth above all by 'knowledge' (*gnosis*), i.e. by demonstrations of their 'spiritual' experiences and by their profound explanations of the 'mysteries' of God?

They certainly had nothing to do with Paul, and it is probable that they had come to Corinth to counteract his influence there. They told the Corinthians that he was not a real apostle: his letters may make a good impression from a distance, they remarked, but once he is with you he is weak; he lacks the gift of eloquence. He is fickle and keeps changing his plans. He has no credentials like ours, so he has to keep on blowing his own trumpet. If he were a real apostle, he would let you support him; after all, the Lord Jesus had himself ordered that his followers should be given hospitality. Paul refuses to accept any. At the same time, though, he is still after your money. He is urging you to contribute to the collection for the Christians in

Jerusalem. Look out for this man, Corinthians, and do not let yourself be taken in!

Some of the new apostles were present at a meeting with the Christians. One of them hurled all kinds of reproaches and accusations at Paul's head. This was bad enough, but the worst thing of all was that the others who were there did not spring to his defence. Paul felt that he had been betrayed by the Christians whom he had so recently called his dear children: 'Though you may have a thousand teachers, you have only one father. I am the one who brought you to life through the gospel.' In these circumstances he could not say any more about the collection for Jerusalem.

Disappointed, he went away northwards, to Macedonia. He did not return to Corinth. Such a visit now no longer made any sense, and it might have been very difficult for him. So he chose Ephesus as his base. From there he planned to write a letter before he came, in order to prepare for another visit in due course.

He did this shortly before he was compelled to leave Ephesus by difficulties which almost cost him his life. Perhaps they were new persecutions, or they may have been the legal proceedings about which he wrote to his friends in Philippi. We do not know. In any case, he wrote his letter 'out of great distress and anxiety, and with many tears'. He gave the letter to his companion Titus. Titus had never been to Corinth before, and he was responsible for the collection in aid of Jerusalem, so he had a very difficult task.

Meanwhile Paul left Ephesus and travelled northwards to the port of Troas, which for some time had also had the status of a Roman colony. On his second journey he had crossed from there to Macedonia. This time he wanted to stay. There were good opportunities for the gospel: it appealed to many people. In Paul's words, 'a door was opened for me in the Lord'. But he was too uneasy to be able to work in Troas for long. Where was Titus? Had his task been too difficult?

Finally Titus came to the community where Paul had been waiting for him (Philippi, Thessalonica?), and gave his report. The Corinthians were deeply affected by the letter which Paul had written in tears. They were very touched. Titus told Paul how sorry they were to have left Paul in the lurch. They had wasted no time in telling his opponent what they thought of him and they intended to take matters further. However, Titus also reported that there were still problems over the collection for Jerusalem.

Titus' report was a great relief to Paul. He could now go on working in Macedonia with more peace of mind. He sent Titus back to Corinth with two other Christians to help him with the work for the collection. He also gave the three of them a letter to deliver.

This letter seems to have been preserved as the first nine chapters of our Second Letter to the Corinthians. After the prayer of thanksgiving, which speaks of the comfort and encouragement given by God in adversity and suffering, Paul explains why he behaved as he did and why he wrote the letter in tears. He asks the Corinthians to deal gently with the person who had so reviled him and goes on to explain how he did not make use of the opportunities which presented themselves in Troas, but went on to Macedonia, because he was disturbed about Titus. Then he suddenly bursts out in a paean of praise to God for the miracle of the proclamation of the gospel. He goes on to develop this theme for several more chapters, obviously with an eye on the question which concerns the Corinthians: how can they recognize a true apostle?

In chapter 7 Paul takes up the thread of his account again: 'When we reached Macedonia there was still no relief for this body of ours: instead there was trouble at every turn. But God, who brings comfort to the downcast, has comforted us by the coming of Titus.' Paul then returns to the consequences of the 'letter in tears' and finally, in chapters 8–9, commends the collection at some length.

The long discussion about the apostleship which is interrupted by Paul's account of his anxiety in Macedonia may be a digression in which he got involved when he was dictating the letter. It is also possible that he dictated this passage separately, and that either he or someone else then inserted it into the letter which he gave to Titus. It does not matter much for our purpose which of the alternatives is the case; either way we can hear Paul talking to the Corinthians in his own words about his work as an apostle and about his personal concerns and those of his colleagues, despite all the opposition and all the disappointment.

I only want to make a few comments on the first part of this section (up to and including chapter 3). To be quite honest, I chose it to show how difficult Paul is for us. Sometimes we have glimpses of a quite alien world of thoughts and imagery behind the words that he uses. Our culture is different from his, and the way in which he deals with his biblical and Jewish heritage is quite unlike our own approach. Finally, the intensely personal way in which he experiences the mystery of Christ's death and resurrection in his apostolic ministry sometimes makes it difficult for us to identify ourselves with him.

'Thanks be to God who, wherever he goes, makes us, in Christ, partners of his triumph and through us is spreading the knowledge of himself, like a sweet smell, everywhere.' As we read this, first of all, we should remember that Paul talks like this at a time of set-backs and difficulties. Only a little while earlier he had written to the Galatians, telling them how the scars on his body from torture were still fresh. Nevertheless, his chief feeling is one of gratitude that he can devote himself so fully to his task. He feels that he is successful, because he describes his work in terms of a victory procession. That, too, is amazing. To an outsider, the result of his preaching was hardly striking: groups of Christians had formed in a number of large cities, but they will not have amounted to more than a few hundred people. Still, Paul regards this as a triumph for Christ, in which he and his fellow workers share.

In the Graeco-Roman world, a great deal of incense was burnt to celebrate triumphal entries and processions. For Paul, the mention of processions calls to mind the smell associated with such events. He uses this fragrance as an image for the knowledge of God which is spread around by those who preach the gospel. This message shows the true nature of God, or rather the way in which he acts towards men: it shows to what lengths he will go to bring men salvation and make them whole.

Paul goes on: 'For we are like a sweet-smelling incense offered by Christ to God, which spreads among those who are being saved and those who are being lost. For those who are being lost, it is a deadly stench that kills; but for those who are being saved, it is a fragrance that brings life.' Paul clearly has two groups of people in mind here: one is on the road to ruin and will get its due deserts on the day of the Lord; the other will finally achieve salvation. He had already made the same point to the Corinthians, when he attacked the way in which they formed partisan groups: 'For the word (the preaching) of the cross is folly to those who are perishing, but to us who are being saved it is the power of God.' Paul has seen often enough how his preaching caused divisions: some people thought that his view that God had chosen to bring about salvation by means of a crucifixion was sheer madness. Others were quite open and felt a completely new power at work in them. Paul seems to think that this division between men is already there when the cross is being preached to them, but he does not develop this germ of predestination.

When he talks of incense instead of fragrance, Paul takes up a different kind of vocabulary, that associated with sacrifice. With a certain amount of background knowledge of the ancient world we can see the associations that a triumphal procession had for Paul, but it is far more difficult for us to see the connection between incense and sacrifice. However, Paul's contemporaries were quite familiar with it. It went without saying that sacrifice was part of worship and that smoke could always be seen rising from the temples. Judaism was no exception here. However, the Jews had what we might call a more 'spiritual' view of sacrifice: it led to communion with God, reconciliation and above all dedication. We use these abstract terms, but the Jews were much more specific. For them the word sacrifice conjured up all kinds of associations: the smoke rising towards God, the thought of renewed communion with him and the smell of the sacrifice itself. When Paul thinks of dedication he often tends to use sacrificial language. While he was in prison in Ephesus, he received a gift from the Philippians which he regarded as a token of their devotion to him and his God; this led him to call it 'a fragrant offering, an acceptable sacrifice, pleasing to God'.

When Paul proclaimed how God acted through the sacrifice of Christ and lived out his message by his mode of life, he believed that people could smell the fragrance of that sacrifice. If they rejected his message and claimed that the crucified Jesus was delivered over to death, then they had an air of putrefaction about them. By contrast, those who accepted Paul's message had a sacrificial fragrance because they shared in the new life of their risen Lord. . .

It was a daunting task and a grave responsibility to confront people with such a definitive decision. 'Who, then, is capable of such a task? We are not like so many others, who handle God's message as if it were cheap merchandise: but because God has sent us, we speak with sincerity in his presence, as servants of Christ.' When I read this sentence, I like to think of the proud way in which Elijah introduces his words: 'Yahweh, in whose presence I stand . . .' These words give a sense of being very close to God, of being open to him and listening only to him. Paul evidently had the same feeling, but he felt close to God because he was 'in Christ'. He contrasts himself with other kinds of apostles. They are not as straightforward as he is, and there are other motives behind their preaching. They water down their wine. This means that it is not so evident that they are handing on God's word, and unlike Paul they need written credentials. 'Does this sound as if we were again boasting about ourselves? Could it be that, like some other people, we need letters of recommendation to you or from you?'

At this point I have to interrupt Paul again, before he tells us how the Corinthian community is in itself a letter of commendation. He does this by using ideas and imagery which are obviously connected and which add up to a coherent picture. The whole area of associations between ideas and imagery is unknown territory, especially for those who are unfamiliar with the Bible. We have already seen something of the way in which Paul talks about how people become Christians. The Corinthians who listened to his preaching were completely changed. God's Spirit gave them new heart and brought them, with Christ, into the new community which Paul can describe as 'the body of Christ'.

The idea that the Corinthian church is itself a testimonial, a letter, and the fact that their hearts have been touched by God's Spirit, reminds Paul of a promise which can be found in chapter 31 of the book of the prophet Jeremiah. The people of Israel had broken the covenant which God had once made with their fore-fathers. Now, through Jeremiah, he promises them a new covenant. But this new covenant will no longer be associated with a law which God has to pronounce. No, 'I will put my law within them, and I will write it upon their hearts.'

Another prophet, Ezekiel, had expressed a similar promise in a rather different way (in chapters 11 and 36): 'I will take out of your flesh the heart of stone and give you a heart of flesh.' This saying refers back to the old covenant made on Sinai, when God's law was handed down on tablets of stone; the new covenant is to be inscribed on men's own hearts. Now we can go on listening to Paul and see how he corrects himself: if the Corinthians are his testimonial, it has been written by Christ himself, through his service.

'You yourselves are the letter we have, written on your hearts for everyone to know and read. It is clear that Christ himself wrote this letter and sent it by us. It is written, not with ink but with the Spirit of the living God, and not on stone tablets but on human hearts.'

Paul finds it incredible that the Corinthians can, through his work as an apostle, be living witnesses to the new covenant. He has been at work, but it is no thanks to him that he is able to act as he does. In his preaching he may confront people with a final decision: salvation or damnation, life or death. He may 'found' a community of the redeemed. Nevertheless, what he achieves does not come about through his own power; it is all the work of God. 'It is he who made us capable of serving the new covenant, which consists not of a written law but of the Spirit. The written law brings death, but the Spirit gives life.'

Before we see how Paul develops the contrast between the written law and the Spirit, we need to remember two things. In Christ God has opened up his new way to mankind and their new way to him. Any other way leads to death, even if that way is a matter of following the Torah. When Paul wrote to the

Galatians, he did more than stress the transitory character of the Torah; he gave reasons why this was inevitable. The Law lays down regulations and condemns those who break them. Its written precepts cannot give life; they only lead to a death sentence. That letter kills.

Secondly, we have also seen how Paul contrasts the hearts of the Corinthians, in which Christ's testimonial has been written, with the 'stone tablets' on which the Torah was inscribed. Here Paul was recalling the famous account in the book of Exodus (chapters 32–34): Moses was given the Law on two stone tablets; he broke them when he found the people dancing round the golden calf, but then climbed Sinai and was given two new tablets in their place. Paul uses only some of the elements in this story and does not go into all its details. One of these elements is that when Moses came down the mountain with the new tablets of stone he 'did not know that the skin of his face shone'. The rather strange verb in the Hebrew text is derived from the word 'horn', which is why the earlier translations said that Moses had horns on his forehead. The translation influenced pictures and statues of Moses, including the famous marble statue made by Michelangelo. However, such pictures are misleading. What the story is trying to convey is that God's conversation with Moses made its mark on him, and indicated something of the force of the divine glory. It dazzled the Israelites so much that Moses had to put a veil over his face when he talked with God. Whenever he went into the tent of meeting to talk again with God, he took the veil off, or, as the Greek can also be translated, the veil was removed from his face.

Remembering all this, Paul goes on to develop his theme, the 'glory' of the office entrusted to his fellow workers, which is that much more glorious than the work of Moses.

'The Law was carved in letter on stone tablets, and God's glory appeared when it was given. Even though the brightness on Moses' face was fading, it was so strong that the people of Israel could not keep their eyes fixed on him. If the Law, which brings death when it is in force, came with such glory, how much greater is the glory that belongs to the activity of the Spirit! The system which brings condemnation was glorious; how much more glorious is the activity which brings salvation. We may say that because of the far brighter glory now the glory that was so bright in the past is gone. For if there was glory in that which lasted for a while, how much more glory is there in that which lasts for ever!'

In the next paragraph Paul goes on to talk about the 'boldness' which he finds so characteristic of himself and his fellow-workers, and indeed of all Christians. The word can have various shades of meaning, depending on the context in which it is used. Here it again has a sense that we often find in Paul: it expresses the certainty that through Christ we have access to God. We are open to him and therefore can describe openly and clearly what God has done and means to do, without being afraid of anything or anyone. To put it more crudely, the real apostle does not mince matters. The story of the stone tablets seems to indicate that all was not well with Moses, because he had to have a veil on his face. Paul seems to think that Moses had something to hide, namely that the brightness on his face faded when he stopped talking directly to God. He goes on to conclude that even now, Jews have veils over their faces. This is a surprising twist to the argument. Perhaps he arrived at it by brooding over the painful fact that most Jews rejected the new salvation. Of course, his thinking was often based on biblical texts. In Isaiah 29, the prophet refers to the hard-heartedness of Israel by saying that God has covered their heads. Paul seems to have remembered this when he was thinking about the veil on Moses' face. The Jews may read their sacred scriptures (which are called the 'Old Testament [Covenant]' for the first time here), but they fail to see that these proclaim the new salvation quite clearly. They listen to the texts, or read them aloud, but they have a veil over their minds and therefore fail to hear God's voice.

However, Paul goes on, Moses' veil was removed when he turned to the Lord. Is he expressing the hope here that in the end his people will come to understand and turn to Christ as their Lord? Be this as it may, many Jews, including Paul and in fact all the Christians, have taken this step. Moses' face shone whenever he had been talking to God, but this brightness was transitory. In Christ, Christians now have a much more intimate relationship with God, and that is permanent. So they continue to shine, and the closer they come to God, the greater their glory, so that because of their communion with Christ they are increasingly filled with the Spirit.

'Because we have this hope, we are very bold. We are not like Moses, who had to put a veil over his face so that the people of Israel would not see the brightness fade and disappear. Their minds, indeed, were closed; and to this very day their minds are covered with the same veil as they read the books of the old covenant. The veil is removed only when a person is joined to Christ. Even today, whenever they read the Law of Moses, the veil still covers their minds. But it can be removed, as the scripture says about Moses: "His veil was removed when he turned to the Lord." Now, "the Lord" in this passage is the Spirit; and where the Spirit of the Lord is present, there is freedom. All of us, then, reflect the glory of the Lord with uncovered faces; and that same glory, coming from the Lord, who is the Spirit, transforms us into his likeness in an ever greater degree of glory.'

When I have read this elated conclusion I have often been asked, Did Paul say all this because it was what he believed? Was he certain that things had to be like this? Did he see Christians in clouds of 'glory' because he was a believer? Or, to put it more bluntly: is this passage just a piece of fanciful theology? Here, too, I think that Paul is drawing on his own experience. We know how people can be transformed and glow when they are really happy, and Paul must have seen this reflected on the faces of newly converted Christians. Perhaps this transforming glow may have gone still deeper with some of them as the years went by.

At the end of chapter 6, after a long passage about the apostolate, we find a passage which seems to have been written by someone else. Paul is talking to the Corinthians, his 'children', in very emotional terms:

'On our part there is no constraint . . . open wide your hearts to us.' Then suddenly there is an appeal to avoid any contact with outsiders:

Do not unite yourselves with unbelievers; they are no fit mates for you. What has righteousness to do with wickedness? Can light consort with darkness? Can Christ agree with Belial, or a believer join hands with an unbeliever? Can there be a compact between the temple of God and the idols of the heathen?

There follows a series of quotations from the Old Testament, introduced in a different way from Paul's usual approach. Then a conclusion is drawn from them, again in terms which are unusual for Paul:

Let us therefore cleanse ourselves from all that can defile flesh or spirit, and in the fear of God complete our consecration.

After this Paul goes on with his emotional words to the Corinthians as though nothing had happened. He had said, 'Open wide your hearts to us', and goes on, 'Do make a place for us . . .'

The digression may come from Paul himself. He often changes the subject suddenly. It is also possible that someone has inserted part of another of his letters here, for example from his earliest letter to Corinth, which is now lost. He himself tells us that in it he had said that the Corinthians should have no dealings with evildoers. But the style of the digression points to someone other than Paul. Since the discovery of the Essene community by the Dead Sea and their writings, scholars have noted how 'Essene' the insertion sounds, not only in content, but also in style and in the choice of biblical texts. The Essenes tended to regard themselves as children of light and avoided any contact with the children of darkness (whose commander they called Belial or Beliar). They formed the holy *ecclesia* of God in the wilderness far from the godless world; they were the people of the new covenant, the living temple in which God dwelt, and all their attention was focussed on the world to come. We can speculate about this to our heart's content. The writer of this passage may have been an Essene from Palestine who was converted to Christianity. In Corinth he may have argued for a closed church community, and perhaps he was so successful that his call to leave the evil world behind found a place in one of Paul's letters at the very point where Paul was concerned about openness . . .

The four chapters at the end of the 'second' letter (10–13) form a section which might be entitled 'Paul's self-defence'. Here he deals with the reproaches and accusations which had been directed against him by the 'apostles' who came to Corinth from elsewhere, and to whom the Corinthian Christians had evidently offered little resistance. This passage does not fit in very well with the first part (1–9). Is it perhaps part of the earlier letter which was written 'in tears'? Or did Paul dictate this section later, after the letter which he had given to Titus and the two Christians from Macedonia?

Whatever the case may be, in this passage Paul seems especially unattractive to modern readers. He talks about himself even more than elsewhere, and does so in a way which appears to us to be arrogant, boastful, overbearing and downright authoritarian. Although he makes this impression on us, perhaps he seemed different to the Corinthians to whom he was writing. They were more familiar with what he believed, how he felt and thought and the way in which he expressed himself.

To be fair to Paul, we should really try to understand all this a little better. I suggest that we might do this by means of a theme which Paul discusses not only here, but also in other letters: the way in which he talks about his 'sufferings', about what he has to endure in order to accomplish his life's work, founding Christian communities in the Gentile world.

The 'apostles' who have come to Corinth call themselves the 'servants' of Christ. Paul responds to their claim by saying that he is even more a servant than they are. 'I have worked much harder, I have been in prison more times, I have been whipped much more, and I have been near death more often.' He then fills in the details in the following summary:

Five times I was given the thirty-nine lashes by the Jews; three times I was whipped by the Romans, and once I was stoned; I have been in three shipwrecks, and once I spent twenty-four hours in the water. In my many trials I have been in danger from floods and from robbers, in danger from fellow Jews and from Gentiles; there have been dangers in the cities, dangers in the wilds, dangers on the high seas, and dangers from false friends. There has been work and toil; often I have gone without sleep; I have been hungry and thirsty; often I have been without enough food, shelter, or clothing.

For the Corinthians none of this was new. When Paul's 'first' letter had been read out, they had heard him criticizing their self-confident attitude. You are proud of all your spiritual gifts and feel that you are perfect Christians; meanwhile we apostles work away, to everyone's utter contempt. 'We go hungry and thirsty and in rags; we are roughly handled; we wander from place to place; we wear ourselves out working with our own hands. They curse us . . . persecute us . . . slander us . . . We are treated as the scum of the earth, the dregs of humanity.'

The Corinthians had also heard this kind of summary elsewhere. It follows a style which was often used in popular philosophy, listing a whole series of tests which the ideal wise man was able to pass. It may sound somewhat exaggerated and overstated to us, because it was borrowed from the rhetoric of the time.

But Paul's Jewish background also comes to the fore here. First of all his words are reminiscent of biblical rhetoric, especially that of the psalms. They describe human distress in very vivid terms, sometimes exaggerating the situation so much that it is impossible to discover the precise nature of the suffering of the person or group concerned. So, for example, someone exclaims in Psalm 22, 'Many bulls have come about me, bulls of Basan have closed me in on every side; they open wide their mouths at me, like a ravening and roaring lion.' And in Psalm 44, the people present this picture of their distress to God: 'For your sake have we been killed all the day long, we have been treated as cattle for the slaughter.'

151

Paul was very familiar with these old prayers, and so he tended to see all the deprivation and ill-treatment and opposition that he endured in terms of them and to use their language to express his feelings.

I have already mentioned how in his discussion of the resurrection Paul talks about his 'fight with wild beasts at Ephesus'. Here he seems to be using the language of the psalms, as he does in the comment that comes immediately before it: 'We (apostles) are in danger every hour. I die daily . . .'

We may call this apparently exaggerated way of speaking 'biblical rhetoric' but that does not mean that we have understood it fully. Other elements of Paul's Jewish background also play a part here. Before the time of the Maccabees, Jews already thought and prayed a good deal about the suffering that some of the faithful evidently had to endure, because, as in the case of Job, it seemed undeserved. This was the time, in the second century BC, when people began to look forward to a new world that God would create. Old ideas were given new forms. God would not content himself with allowing his faithful to be put to the test by hostility and suffering, and then reward them more richly later on in their lives. On the contrary, God was now making suffering itself a clear indication that those who had to undergo it would have a part in the coming new world.

Suffering for the sake of righteousness, for God's sake, now became a sign of election. After all, the prophets whom God had sent in former days had also been persecuted and killed by evil men. Because of this, it was thought particularly important to bear suffering bravely, and they were even glad to suffer.

Moreover, it was thought that terrifying manifestations of evil directed against the faithful would be the prelude to the great day of salvation. The righteous would be tried almost beyond endurance. In some circles people called these last perils the 'birthpangs of the Messiah'. Violent persecution was thus a sign that the ultimate redemption was at hand. That was another reason for remaining profoundly happy despite all the suffering.

For Christians, all these notions took on a new content. The evil powers of the old world had done their worst to Jesus, the Righteous One *par excellence*, and had inflicted the most appalling suffering and death on him. The Messiah had undergone the ultimate tortures in person, and now lived in God's glory. Those who took up his cause, who wanted to be among his followers, had to undergo persecution and suffering for his sake. But now they could do that boldly and even be happy about it: their reward would be great in heaven.

Paul was familiar with all this, but he believed it, thought it through and expressed it in his own distinctive way. We have often heard him describe how his whole life is governed by Christ. For Paul, the fact that Christ has died and risen again is not just an event from the past; it is something that continues to have an influence and to exercise power in his own life. It also gives strength to all Christians, who have to endure persecution and deprivation wherever Paul 'plants' the new way of life. They are following in the steps of Jesus, who endured sufferings caused by the same powers of evil. It is from the risen Lord that Paul receives strength to carry on preaching and founding new communities, 'outspokenly', boldly, and with joy. To his friends in Philippi he wrote that he had given away his privileges as a Jew, counting them as mere garbage, because he only wanted to live for and with Christ.

All I want is to know Christ and to experience the power of his resurrection; to share in his sufferings and become like him in his death, in the hope that I myself will be raised from death to life.

This kind of dying and rising with Christ ought to be evident in the attitudes and behaviour of a true apostle. In chapter 4 of the letter which Paul gave to Titus to bring to the Corinthians from Macedonia, he writes:

We are often troubled, but not crushed; sometimes in doubt, but never in despair; there are many enemies, but we are never without a friend; and though badly hurt at times, we are not destroyed. At all times we carry in our mortal bodies the death of Jesus, so that his life also may be seen in our bodies. Throughout our lives we are always in danger of death for Jesus' sake, in order that his life may be seen in this mortal body of ours.

Further on, in chapter 6, Paul again gives a summary of the deprivations, the needs and the sorrows that 'we apostles' endure, contrasting them with the power of God which is at work. He concludes:

We are treated as liars, yet we speak the truth; as unknown, yet we are known by all; as though we were dead, but, as you see, we live on. Although punished, we are not killed; although saddened, we are always glad; we seem poor, but we make many people rich; we seem to have nothing, yet we really possess everything.

In presenting his equivalent to the 'credentials' which the newly-arrived apostles can show to the Corinthians, Paul again and again points to the only credible hallmark of the true apostle: others must be able to see his life 'in the flesh' as a reflection of his crucified Lord. This life is shot through with suffering, pain, care, poverty, and 'dying', yet at the same time Christ's own life can be seen at work there.

—➤12➤—

Romans: On the Way to the End

Paul's Jewish past caused difficulties for him. It was a nagging pain to him that his own people had remained so stubborn in the face of the declared will of their God. Paul felt that there could be no doubt that this will was explicit and blindingly clear, because it had been revealed to him by Israel's God in person. The crucified Jesus was God's Messiah, his Son, the Lord, and that meant that God had come to all men in an unheard-of new way.

It was no less painful to Paul that Jews who recognized Jesus as Messiah still could not accept that their Gentile fellow-believers had equal rights. They continued to avoid Gentiles because they thought that they were 'unclean', and some of them even tried to present the Jewish way of life as a necessity for salvation. Paul's preaching in the Gentile world sometimes led to the formation of a new community 'in Christ', but no sooner had he left them than Jewish Christians came along to trouble the young believers, often deliberately acting against Paul.

It was perhaps because of all this that he arrived at the remarkable and, one might almost say, contradictory plan which finally led to his death. He probably decided on it during the three months when he stayed in Corinth after being in Macedonia (probably in AD 56). Relationships with the Christians there had been improved by the letter which Titus and his companions had taken and perhaps also through other contacts. This was Paul's third stay in the city, following the eighteen months he had spent establishing the community (AD 50–51) and the short, painful visit from Ephesus (AD 54), and it was definitely the last. It was his farewell visit.

He had made his plans: he wanted to take the gospel to the western part of the Roman empire, beginning in Spain. He wanted to work a long way away, among people who had not yet heard the name of Christ, and where Jewish sympathizers would not keep interfering. He would go there via Rome. The Christian community in Rome was to be the base for his new enterprise.

That was one half of his plan. But before he went to Rome, he wanted first to go to the other capital, Jerusalem, the centre of Jewish life. A group of Christians was to travel there as a delegation from Paul's churches, which had zealously collected money for the poor Christians of Jerusalem. Paul had decided to go with them. This might seem a contradiction in his plan. He wanted to go to the West, far from the Jewish agitation against him, but before that he was going to put his head in the lion's den and travel to Jerusalem.

We can discover this from Paul's letter to the Romans, which he dictated to a secretary called Tertius during his last stay in Corinth. Of all the letters that have come down to us, this is the longest, and it is also the only one to a community which Paul himself had not founded. It was extremely important for Paul to prepare for his visit to Rome in this way. His new plan to bring the gospel to Spain would have little chance of success without a flourishing Christian community as a base. He needed the same kind of support as Antioch had once given him.

The community in Rome was certainly flourishing. When I described Paul's encounter with the Jewish couple Aquila and Prisca in Corinth, I mentioned that there were Christians in Rome towards the end of the forties. In AD 49 or 50, the emperor Claudius had expelled from the city a number of the chief agitators in the dispute about Chrestus. As a result, non-Jewish Christians may well have formed a majority in the community there. However, after the death of the emperor in AD 54, the number of Jews doubtless began to increase, and Jewish Christians will also have become more numerous. The church in Rome was a flourishing community, but it is also certain that Paul was a controversial figure for it. The Jewish world which remained faithful to traditional belief saw him as a traitor to Israel, an apostate. Moreover, he had involved so many other people in his sins that the sooner he was taken care of, the better. He was doubtless the subject of a good deal of talk in the synagogues of Rome.

Jews who had been converted and who believed in Jesus as the Messiah also disagreed with his radical view that Gentiles were accepted by God as his children simply through their belief in Christ. For Paul, Gentiles had precisely the same opportunities as Jews, no less and no more. In Christ all the earlier differences had disappeared.

The Jewish Christians had so much difficulty with this radical view of Paul's that they would believe and pass on all kinds of slander about him. He was said to have called the Torah 'sinful'. He was thought to encourage immorality: if there is no more law, anything goes. He was said to hate his own people because he argued that God had definitely rejected them. In other words, God had broken faith with those who believed in him. What blasphemy!

Paul has all these Jewish objections in mind as he dictates his letter for the Christians in Rome to Tertius. It is now several months since he sent his plea for the Spirit to the Galatians, and since then he has been thinking hard. He is more aware than anyone else of the difficulties which the Jews have with his gospel, because he himself was such an ardent Jew. As he dictates, he sometimes seems to be carrying on a conversation with a particular Jew, perhaps his former self. This running conversation sometimes makes his argument difficult to understand. We have already seen that quotation marks were unknown in Paul's day; consequently in some sentences we cannot be sure who is speaking, Paul or his conversation partner. Moreover, when we looked at the letter to the Galatians, we already saw how much more difficult Paul is to understand when he talks and argues in Jewish fashion, 'to the Jews I became as a Jew'.

There is another important point. It is much more difficult for us western Christians to read the letter to the Romans in an unbiassed way than any of the other letters we have considered. Over the centuries it has had enormous influence on our thought and beliefs which we find it very difficult to escape. Let me just mention two aspects of this. First of all there is the role which the letter began to play at the time of the Reformation. At that time Christians began to pay a great deal of attention to the soul and its salvation, to the inner life of the individual. For years Luther wrestled with the fact that he was incapable of fulfilling the demands of the law, that is, obeying all the regulations and prohibitions of the church and his monastic order. In his desperate search for a God who could be gracious to him despite his irresistible temptation to sin, he found what he was looking for in the letter to the Romans: a man is not justified by doing the works of the law, but by grace alone. It seemed as though Paul himself had struggled with the same problem and was the first to have received this saving revelation. So, for example, the seventh chapter of the letter was understood as a description of Paul's experience before his conversion. Elsewhere, too, Paul was thought to have said and experienced things that were unlike him, and quite alien to his view of life.

Secondly, theologians in the West have seen their task primarily as being to interpret the Bible in such a way that its statements add up to a logical and consistent system. In doing this they have, of course, made use of western concepts and patterns of thought, many of which have derived from Greek philosophy. For example, they worked out a doctrine of atonement on the basis of the death of Christ in which some of Paul's sayings were incorporated. This doctrine was set out in dogmas and confessional writings, and some of the terms in which it was expressed became stamped on the minds of believers. As a result, it became impossible to listen to Paul's words without reading the whole of the doctrine into them. In this way, too, Paul was made to say things which he had not intended.

As we read the letter to the Romans, we must try as far as possible to start from Paul and his own concerns. Paul's question was not the same as Luther's: he did not ask how, given his constant tendency to sin, he could find a gracious God and thus bring peace to his soul. Paul sought a justification for the question, 'What is God up to in his dealings with men, and how are we to account for them?' If we begin from Paul, we might put his question in a slightly different way. He asks how he can justify the task he has been given, to incorporate the non-Jewish world, the Gentiles, into God's people without imposing the demands which have hitherto been made, those of circumcision and the Law. But it is better to start from God, because he himself instituted circumcision and the Law when he bound himself for ever to his people Israel?

These were the burning questions for Paul when he began to dictate his letter to the Romans. That is why the address is rather top-heavy. Paul tells the Romans that he has been set apart by God for his gospel. But they are not to think that this means that in the gospel God is breaking with his past. His prophets have already proclaimed the gospel in the scriptures. It concerns his Son Jesus, and here too it is not a break with what has gone before. Paul seldom mentions the fact that humanly speaking Jesus was an Israelite by descent. He is, however, familiar with the confession of faith made by Jewish Christians, which states that Jesus was born of the seed of David, that he was Son of God, and was raised from the dead. Paul accepts this confession, though he has his own way of putting it. Finally, on the authority of God himself he accepts non-Jews into his community without obliging them to obey the Torah. This, too, is not really a break with the past. The new way, the way of faith, does not give anyone *carte blanche* to do as he likes; faith also requires obedience.

I have gone through the whole of Romans with my group in this way, trying as far as possible to show what Paul means, in his own terms. As before, at times he seemed to move away from us, and at other times he came very near. In this short book I shall have to limit myself to a few comments on Paul's arguments without going into much detail on individual passages.

Paul describes the gospel as 'the saving power of God for every-one who has faith – the Jew first, but the Greek (the non-Jew) also'. Here Paul speaks from experience. He himself has seen its power at work, among Gentiles just as much as among Jews. He is, however, troubled by the question as to the degree to which the Jews have priority, hence the remarkable insertion of the word 'first'. We may well be surprised at what comes next. This powerful gospel is a revelation of God's righteousness. We might have expected Paul to call it a revelation of God's love for all men, of his boundless mercy. To us the word righteousness suggests a judge who pronounces his verdict according to the law, without allowing his personal feelings to enter into it.

Here again we come up against a way of thinking which is alien to us. For us, legal terms are indeed impersonal. There is a body of law which all of us have to observe, including the judge who condemns infringements of it. Sometimes Paul thinks in the same way. But in addition (and occasionally at the same time), we find a different way of looking at the law which he has inherited from the Old Testament. In the Old Testament world, justice was administered by the king. He was not bound to an impersonal body of law, so that he could act 'outside the law' and be influenced by his personal feelings towards his subjects. The best thing I can do here is to point to chapters 40—55 of the book of Isaiah. Here we can see the connection between the proclamation of the good news (the gospel) that God is going to demonstrate his justice and the way in which it is understood as salvation, as deliverance for his people. In this text, the good news is for the remnants of God's defeated people. The new element in Paul's gospel is that God means to give his righteousness, i.e. his salvation, his deliverance, to *all* men.

'God's righteousness' has now been 'revealed', i.e. has been made visible, to believers. Paul goes on to use the same word in connection with 'God's wrath'. He sees the utter corruption of the entire Gentile world as a divine punishment. His description of this seems less strange when we read contemporary Jewish writings. We can imagine how a Jew listening to Paul's judgment on the Gentiles would nod his head in agreement. And of course he would have been very cross when Paul concluded: 'You Jews are no better.'

As we know, Paul was so blinded by the light from Christ that everything outside it seemed to him to be pitch dark. He discovered texts from the Bible that said the same thing: nobody does good. However, despite the fact that the power of sin is so widespread, there is nowhere to which the new salvation given to us by God in Christ does not extend (chapter 3).

When Paul goes on to talk about the message of Christ, he uses language from the world of Jewish sacrifice: 'whom God put forward as an expiation by his blood'. Although the world of sacrifice will always seem strange to us, we can get some idea of it from Leviticus, chapter 16. This describes what is to be done on the great day of atonement. We can see clearly from it what significance the Jews attached to blood. For them, blood was the mysterious life-force itself, which came from God. That is why from time immemorial they used it in those rites which expressed their bond, their communion with God. According to the account in Exodus 24, the covenant on Sinai was concluded in blood. Half the blood from the sacrificial animals was sprinkled on the altar, which represented God, and half was sprinkled on the people present. This expressed the living relationship between God and people. In Leviticus 16, the cover over the ark of the covenant is to be sprinkled with blood, because this is what represents God here. We need not bother with the details of the ritual; the important thing to remember is that God himself has ordained all this. Each year, he gives his people the opportunity of renewing their relationship with him, assuring them that he will not hold against them the sins that they have committed during the past year. Paul will have had the main features of this ritual at the back of his mind when he reflected on what he had seen in so many others: by the death of Christ, God had entered into a new relationship with men, a new covenant. Because of it, he had drawn a line, not just under the previous year but under the whole of the past, and made a new start.

One more thing. Although for Paul everything that happens before and apart from Christ is so dark, so utterly beyond redemption, Paul does not see Christ as the climax of a history of salvation. In this he differs from some of the other New Testament writers and those modern authors who see the Old Testament as a record of the ongoing development of Israelite belief over the centuries. In the dark ages before Christ, Abraham is the only figure who shines out. He is not, however, seen as the starting point for a history of faith, but as the 'father' of the

161

Christian community which is to emerge many centuries later. Paul looks at things like this because he is talking to Jews. They call themselves 'children of Abraham', and because of this they regard themselves as the people of God. Paul's task is now to form, in Christ, a new people which will be made up of both Jews and uncircumcised Gentiles. Abraham was associated so closely with the idea of the people of God that Paul was virtually forced to consider his significance. Fortunately for him, the book of Genesis records that Abraham was a believer and received the promises before he was circumcised. Because of this, Paul can refer to him as the father of the new community. He develops this point more deeply than he did in the letter to the Galatians, virtually identifying Abraham's faith with that of the Christians; it is surrender to the God 'who gives life to the dead and calls into existence the things that do not exist' (chapter 4).

One other figure in the Bible is important for Paul, but he does not come from Israel's past. This is Adam, the father of mankind. With him, man's troubles began. Paul contrasts Adam with Christ, who marks the beginning of a new humanity; he is not so much their ancestor as their living source of life (chapter 5).

This new humanity lives from Christ, freed from the deadly power of the Law, but that does not mean that they do what they like, as a Jew might fear. On the contrary, those who live in communion with the Lord who died and rose again can use the same terms as a zealous Jew to describe their way of living. It is life before God, in complete obedience to him and in his service (chapter 6). This leads Paul to consider the value of the Law, a question which has already arisen on a number of occasions. In his impassioned letter to the Galatians he had taken a very negative view of the Law, whereas for Jews it was God's greatest gift to his people. Now Paul concedes that the Torah comes from God and is therefore holy; it is meant for man's well-being. It has such a deadly force because man himself is in the power of sin. Although he is deeply concerned to do good, he always fails. Going over into the first person, Paul describes the inner contradiction which so torments men. In this dramatic passage we feel

162

that he is very near to us (chapter 7). Perhaps that is even more the case in the next chapter, when he describes what happens when the Spirit moves a man to the depths of his being (chapter 8).

This chapter is one of the most telling passages in the whole Bible. Over the centuries, countless Christians have learnt parts of it off by heart. Time and again it has given them strength not to give up hope. Paul begins with a contrast between 'flesh' and 'spirit' which we have already come across in the letter to the Galatians; now, however, he develops it in connection with what he has just been saying about sin and the Law. As in Galatians, he argues that Christians are no longer slaves, no longer subjects of the powers of death, but true sons of God and therefore, with Christ, 'heirs'. But here he also says that fear is the mark of those who are still bound up in 'the flesh', in slavery. By fear, Paul means that anxiety which comes to all of us when we realize our true situation: that we, our friends and our children, are bound to die, that what we have done will be forgotten, and that everything is useless. That is, unless we can escape from this fate, from the transitoriness of all things.

Let me quote part of the chapter. Note how Paul begins with the third person, 'all who', and then moves through the second person, 'you have', to the first, 'we are'. It is obviously the words 'Abba! Father!' which make him think of praying together ('we'); the exclamation of trust has a powerful effect as the cry of God's own Spirit, welling up from deep inside us.

'For all who are led by the Spirit of God are sons of God. For you did not receive the spirit of slavery to fall back into fear, but you have received the spirit of sonship. When we cry, "Abba! Father!" it is the Spirit himself bearing witness with our spirit that we are children of God, and if children, then heirs, heirs of God and fellow heirs with Christ, provided we suffer with him in order that we may also be glorified with him.'

The suffering, Paul goes on, bears no comparison with the glory that is to come. We have already come across the word several times. In the Old Testament, 'glory' is mostly used in connection with God. Old Testament writers sometimes describe how God's mysterious presence could be seen in the form of a blinding light, his 'glory'. For Paul, a man is perfected when he is completely filled with the presence of God. Only Jesus is perfect in this way. Because we are believers and share in the Spirit, we too have a burning desire for this perfection. Moreover, Paul continues, this desire can be found throughout creation. Once again, this remarkable argument goes back to the world of the Old Testament. There nature is closely associated with man's relationship to God. When that is broken, the earth becomes a wilderness and brings forth thorns and thistles. When God intervenes to save his people, the trees clap their hands and the mountains begin to dance. Now that God has perfected one man, Jesus, and has joined the hearts of believers to him by giving them the pledge of the Spirit, the whole of creation longs for final freedom from decay.

It sighs and groans with us, Paul says, who have the first fruits of the Spirit and long for the redemption of our bodies. This is what Paul dictated according to the oldest copy of Romans that we possess. At a later stage, 'adoption as sons' was inserted before 'redemption of our bodies', evidently because Christians thought that the latter phrase did not say enough. They had ceased to understand how important the body was for Paul; it was the only basis on which men could come together.

Paul became more and more elated as he went on dictating. When people become Christians, God begins a process in them that he will carry through to the end, however wretched and guilty and oppressed and shattered they themselves may feel. For when God loves anyone, nobody and nothing can part them from his love.

As he gets carried away, Paul's style changes. Explanations and arguments give place to questions, which end up in a kind of victory cry. 'Rhetorical questions', we might say, recalling a form of which Paul is particularly fond. Or perhaps at the same time they reflect whatever doubts had at times pressed in on him. The summary of everything that threatens 'us' amounts to a description of what an apostle had to endure, as we know from Paul's remarks elsewhere. Hence his quotation from the psalms. Later Christians have rightly applied his words to all the sickness and pain and violence that we have to endure in this world of 'the flesh'. These are the powers of evil which he mentions at the end of the passage. But let him speak for himself.

'What then shall we say to this? If God is for us, who is against us? He who did not spare his own Son but gave him up for us all, will he not also give us all things with him? Who shall bring any charge against God's elect? It is God who justifies; who is to condemn? It is Christ Jesus who died, yes, who was raised from the dead, who is at the right hand of God, who indeed intercedes for us. Who shall separate us from the love of Christ? Shall tribulation, or distress, or persecution, or famine, or nakedness, or peril, or sword? As it is written, "For thy sake we are being killed all the day long; we are regarded as sheep to be slaughtered." No, in all these things we are more than conquerors through him who loved us. For I am sure that neither death, nor life, nor angels, nor principalities, nor things present, nor things to come, nor powers, nor height, nor depth, nor anything else in all creation, will be able to separate us from the love of God in Christ Jesus our Lord.'

In chapters 9–11 Paul deals with the problem of Israel's unbelief. The fact is that, to Paul's distress, Israel as a whole has rejected the new perspective which has been opened up by God. Paul acknowledges the election of Israel and the privileges which that involves. But as a Jew who believes in the Bible he also has to acknowledge that God is free to make up 'Israel' from anyone whom he cares to choose. He can select Abraham's physical descendants, a 'remnant' of Israel, but he can also choose those whom he first called 'not my people', i.e. Gentiles. And this is what he has in fact done. The message of the new salvation has reached all the Jews, but the great majority of them continue to seek their salvation in the Torah. They have refused to believe, and have rejected Christ. As a consequence of this, God is compelled to extend to other nations the infinite mercy which he cannot bestow on Israel. However, the Gentiles who are thus favoured must sense that through this grace they really are incorporated into God's people: for example, they are like wild figs grafted on to the tree of Israel. They certainly cannot turn up their noses at God's own stubborn people.

Paul then ventures a prophetic vision of God's plan, which is a 'mystery': according to a saying of Moses himself, the fact that God's grace has been bestowed so generously on so many Gentiles is meant to make Israel jealous. God plans to move the Israelites so deeply that they come to accept God's mercy of their own accord. Here Paul turns upside down a vision of the future which had been prominent in Jewish tradition: God would first glorify his own people, and then all the other nations, the Gentiles, would travel to Sion to find salvation there.

If this is what God intends, says Paul, then it seems that my preaching among the Gentiles is even more important than I imagined: I am helping to make the Jews jealous, and so I am really working for their conversion, which is essential for the ultimate salvation of all mankind. So my preaching among the Gentiles is a help to Israel.

There is no doubt that Paul was very concerned about his people. Perhaps he suffered more than anyone else because of their blindness to the new salvation in which the God of Israel had granted him a unique share. He must have pondered deeply on the theme of God and Israel for a long time before he dictated this section to Tertius (if he had not done so earlier on another occasion). But he leaves us asking how this vision of the role of Israel is to be combined with his express belief that 'in Christ' the distinction between Jew and Gentile is done away with for good. How can there still be a place for a separate role for Israel in this new and definitive community?

When we consider this question we must remember that Paul expected that God's plans would soon be fulfilled. He himself, or at any rate his contemporaries, would share in the great consummation. He could not have supposed that human history would continue, century after century, for twenty centuries, with Christians living alongside Jews for all this time.

After Paul has outlined his vision of God's plan for Israel, he ends with a number of exclamations which really amount to a hymn of praise for the unfathomable nature of this mystery. It is an object lesson for those believers who have felt that they could say something about God's plan with one man, one people, his world.

How great are God's riches! How deep are his wisdom and knowledge! Who can explain his decisions? Who can understand his ways? As the scripture says, 'Who knows the mind of the Lord? Who is able to give him advice? Who has ever given him anything, so that he had to pay it back?' For all things were created by him, and all things exist through him and for him. To God be the glory forever! Amen.

Paul ends his letter with various pieces of advice (chapters 12–15). One of them begins like this: 'Every person must submit to the supreme authorities. There is no authority but by act of God, and the existing authorities are instituted by him; consequently anyone who rebels against authority is resisting a divine institution, and those who so resist have themselves to thank for the punishment they will receive.' That means, Paul goes on, that Christians are to do their duty as citizens and to pay taxes and tolls. The authorities responsible for this are in God's service.

This is one of those passages after which Paul would have written 'Read this and burn it', had he suspected how Christians would make use of this statement to justify evil regimes. Of course, this thought never occurred to him, because he expected the end of the world very soon: Christ the Lord would come quickly and sit in judgment. That is why he dictated this advice to the Christians in Rome, in their particular situation. He knew how precarious it was.

Jews had been banished from Rome by the emperor Claudius, but they were allowed to return in 54, after his death, when Nero came to power. Of course they had to take care not to attract the watchful attention of the authorities once again by quarrelling among themselves. This also went for those Jews who had embraced the new faith and who joined in house meetings with uncircumcised Christians. These were the groups to whom Paul was writing here. They had to be careful not to provoke oppressive police action. Paul also knew that the Roman authorities were very favourably disposed towards citizens who gave proof of their loyalty. At the same time, however, he was well aware that it was particularly difficult for those who lived in Rome to be loyal. The historian Tacitus tells us that during the first years of Nero's rule the population in the city and the provinces suffered increasingly under the corrupt system of taxation. He describes the rapacity of the *publicani*, the tax-farmers appointed by the state, who demanded far more money than they were due. In 58, Tacitus reports, the people protested so vigorously that Nero, always impulsive, hit on the idea of abolishing all indirect taxes. His council, however, talked him out of it, having first praised the grandeur of his conception. This was in 58; Paul dictated his letter in 56.

Paul advises the Romans to pay taxes and tolls, no matter how difficult it may be for them. He gives reasons both here and in the preceding chapter. He has just been talking about the love which Christians must show not only to one another but also to everyone outside their group. 'If possible, so far as it lies with you, live at peace with all men. My dear friends, do not seek revenge, but leave a place for divine retribution; for there is a text which reads, "Justice is mine, says the Lord, I will repay." ' Paul seems to be suggesting that this also applies to the authorities about whom he is going on to speak!

Paul adopts a view of state authority which had been developed by the Jewish thinkers of his day. The ruler or king is in God's service. When he punishes criminals, he is as it were exercising God's judgment. Paul concludes, 'Therefore one must be subject, not only to avoid God's wrath but also for the sake of conscience.' In making this remark, if I understand him rightly, he means something like this. Do not take any action as a community against the authority of the state; whenever the state intervenes it does so in God's name, which means that you draw down the wrath of God upon yourselves. At the same time, do not act as a result of your own assessment of the situation, because of your conscience. Two things are important for you. First, there is your obligation as Christians to demonstrate your love .and desire for peace to outsiders, and secondly there is the certainty that before long the Lord himself will appear and pass judgment.

At the end of his letter to the Romans Paul says something

about his plans to visit Spain and the support for it which he hopes to get from the Christians in Rome. Then he comes to the collection for the poor in Jerusalem. He himself wants to go with those who are taking it, and is well aware of the risks that he runs:

I implore you by our Lord Jesus Christ and by the love that the Spirit inspires, to be my allies in the fight; pray to God for me that I may be saved from unbelievers in Judaea, and that my errand to Jerusalem may find acceptance with God's people.

This collection is already familiar to us. Paul mentioned it earlier when he was talking to the Galatians about his conversations with James and Peter in Jerusalem. No Jewish obligations at all were to be imposed on Gentiles who became Christians, but Paul and Barnabas were to ask the converts to 'remember' the poor Christians in Jerusalem – in other words, to give them financial support.

We can easily imagine why many of the converted Jews in Jerusalem were in financial straits. The leading figures, the Twelve, had come from Galilee, where they had once earned a living as fishermen, peasant farmers, or in other humble local occupations. After the 'appearance' of Jesus in Galilee they had returned to Jerusalem. And without doubt they had brought their families with them. There, in the heart of the Jewish world, they had to bear witness to Jesus. There, too, he would soon be revealed as the glorified Son of man, the son of David.

Poor people in Jerusalem who accepted the new faith could no longer count on the philanthropy of the synagogue. We have seen that Luke had heard about a quarrel between two groups of Jewish Christians, the Hellenists and the Hebrews, over 'the daily distribution to the widows'. Moreover, the community felt called to bear witness to Jesus the Messiah outside Jerusalem as well, in Judaea, Samaria and further afield: and the preachers had to take some emergency funds with them.

Paul kept to the agreement. When he appeals in his letters to his communities for the collection for Jerusalem, he gives differing reasons. His own real motive was certainly his struggle for unity among Christians. Those of Jewish origin regarded themselves as a group distinct from former Gentiles. The Gentile Christians did not observe the laws of purity. To have contacts with them and to sit at the same table was certainly not on, especially for the Jewish Christians who lived in Jerusalem and Judaea. The old pattern of life had been too deeply impressed on them. And would there be any changes in the future? No, because there was to be no future: Christ would appear very soon.

The unity of the two groups could be expressed by the alms sent by Paul's communities in the Gentile world. Perhaps Paul was influenced by the pattern of the relationship between the 'God-fearers' and Israel. The God-fearers felt themselves to be at one with the Jews in their confession of the one true God, but they could not accept the Jewish way of life. Despite this difference, they sought to express their common belief by giving the Jews financial support. In the same way, gifts sent by Christians from Macedonia, Greece and Asia might express the fact that the givers felt themselves bound to the 'saints' in Jerusalem in one confession of Jesus as Lord, despite their different ways of life.

But why did Paul not have the offering brought by delegates from the communities, of whom Luke mentions seven by name at the beginning of Acts 20? Why did he himself want to go with them (perhaps as a delegate from Corinth)? He must have known that it would be dangerous for him, and he may also have felt that the Jewish Christians in Jerusalem would rather not see him. Was he influenced by a deep emotional link with his people and the city of God where he was brought up, the very link which suggested to him the amazing divine plan which he describes in the letter to the Romans?

We cannot know. But we do know for sure that things went wrong in Jerusalem. We can read this in Luke's account, from chapter 20 onwards. Paul was arrested in the Temple precinct, remained as a prisoner in Caesarea for two years and then was taken to Rome. Luke indicates that he was aware of Paul's eventual execution, by hinting at it in his moving account of

Paul's farewell in Miletus. But he ends his book with the report that Paul preached the gospel freely and 'unhindered' in Rome.

Paul was executed in Rome under Claudius' successor Nero (AD 54–68). But we do not know in what year that happened, or whether Paul was freed again after the episode described at the end of Acts. Nor can we be at all certain whether he made more journeys or wrote more letters.

Postscript

I have been talking to my 'Paul group' like this about his life and the letters that we can be sure he wrote. I hope that this book has also brought Paul rather closer to the reader, and has shown how different Paul was from us and yet so urgently concerned with the mystery of Christ which is still important today.

When I was reading through the manuscript and came to the mention of my old Volkswagen, I thought how unlike Paul's times were to our own. As I followed the route of his journeys, I went through breathtaking scenery. He must have seen its beauty too, for example in the Taurus mountains, and among the Greek islands. But he says nothing about that. He was constantly threatened by dangers. In that respect, too, he is a stranger to us. He seems only to see the negative side of things, and comes over to us as a pessimist. All the world of 'the flesh' is sinful, without prospects, doomed to death. It is not given to us to enjoy. We miss in Paul the positive feeling for life that is so characteristic of some writers of the Old Testament. Paul was evidently influenced by the pessimistic view of 'this world' which was held by most believing Jews of his time and which was also characteristic of the Graeco-Roman world. Moreover, measured by the light of his experience of Christ, everything else was gloomy.

Paul also seems to have been singularly unmoved by all the inhumanity of his world. We have seen the sufferings that he himself had to endure in the service of Christ, but he says nothing about the manifold sufferings of others. There is not a word about what men endure as a result of natural disasters, contagious diseases, war, and above all as a result of the organization of society (including slavery). He seems unconcerned with all the senseless human suffering which makes belief in a loving God so difficult for modern people.

At this point, someone might object: Paul was well aware of all this, but he expected our sorry world to come to an end soon, and therefore there would be no more suffering and pain. That may well be. But Jesus shared Paul's expectations, and he did his utmost to help the suffering people with whom he came into contact. We can see this from the stories about him told in the four gospels. Here again, we discover a strange thing about Paul: he says remarkably little in his letters about the earthly life of Jesus. It seems as though all the accounts of Jesus' preaching, the miracles he performed and his championing of the outcast, simply passed Paul by. It is true that Paul was dead by the time the four gospels were written, but it is quite certain that the material in them was being handed down in Christian churches. The story of Jesus' ministry was very much alive. Did Paul have little to do with the communities in which it was told? Were they to be found chiefly in Palestine and Syria? Did they consist of simple people in villages and small towns, with whom Paul the intellectual felt little in common? There is yet another possibility that we ought to consider.

Paul is concerned above all with the end and climax of Jesus' earthly life, his death on the cross, through which God bestowed new life, his own life, on men. Paul felt very close to the person of Jesus, the Christ. We saw how in the letter to the Galatians he used the language of love ('it is no longer I who live, but it is Christ who lives in me'). Paul often describes his life as a deepening communion with his crucified and risen Lord. In this 'mystical' union with Christ he experiences the unimaginable love of God. According to his view, God had revealed, made concrete, given form to his love for men by means of Jesus' self-surrender on the cross and his resurrection from the dead. Might it be, then, that everything that Jesus had said and done to reveal God's love during his earthly life had paled into insignificance for Paul in the light of the cross and resurrection? This suggestion seems to me to have much to commend it. Perhaps Paul was also afraid that stories about Jesus' miraculous cures might distract people from the most important things of all: cross, resurrection and the new life in the Spirit; moreover, to hand on Jesus' teaching might lead Christians to regard it as a new Torah, with a righteousness of its own. Could this be why Paul did not bother to use the gospel material, and preferred to keep his distance from it?

Be this as it may, there is a remarkable difference between Paul's approach and that of the gospels. This difference was not noted until the nineteenth century, when scholars began to consider the New Testament 'historically'. Before that, Christians had read it in the light of church doctrine, in which the various texts of the Bible were harmonized and made into a coherent whole. Anyone who came across Paul's mention of 'the gospel' that he preached would understand this to be a reference to the stories in Matthew and the other gospels. Historical criticism, however, demonstrated that this was impossible and pointed to the absence of references to Jesus' earthly life in Paul's letters. Many critics were 'freethinkers'; they, or rather their ancestors, had left the churches and were often unsympathetic to Christian teaching. The more they discovered the 'historical' Jesus who lay behind the texts of the gospels, the more they felt that Paul had really proclaimed a new faith which had nothing to do with the man from Nazareth. Some of them blamed Paul for starting the church system which they so hated. The philosopher Friedrich Nietzsche, with his acute sensitivity to the undercurrents of his time, gave striking expression to that dislike of Paul in a book called *The Antichrist* (1895). In it, he argued that Paul had completely falsified the message of Jesus, turning the good news into bad news. Paul was impelled by hatred, which at the same time was a lust for power. The priest in Paul was trying to get out, which is why he kept using concepts and dogmas which could be used to tyrannize the masses. Paul was aware of the needs of the world of his time. He combined the concepts of sacrifice, guilt and sin with pagan mystery religions, and from this mixture the church came into being.

Nietzsche's views are still repeated in some circles today, but they are based on a misunderstanding. Paul began, not from what Jesus did in his earthly life, but from what *God* did at the end of that life. Because of this, Paul seems to be more of a theologian than the other New Testament writers: he talks more about God. He does so, however, in a way which shows that he never forgets that he is talking about a mystery. He does not think in concepts and definitions and propositions, but in images. He finds them in the rich tradition of Judaism and in all the different human relationships with which he is familiar. Sometimes he uses a variety of images one after another or even one on top of another, and this makes it difficult for us to follow him. It was the theologians of the western church who first set out to arrange in a logical system what the Bible, including Paul, said. This led them, for example, to construct theories about the atonement: God was affronted by sin and required the blood of his Son as satisfaction; a price had to be paid, and there were great arguments as to who exacted it. We might also think of theological discussions of predestination, which have blighted the life of so many Christians. We are now seeing a rebellion against all this, but there is no historical justification whatsoever for laying the blame on Paul.

Paul can irritate us because he is so sure of his faith. Doubt and scepticism have eaten into modern culture. Our religious feelings are not those of Paul and his fellow Christians in the New Testament. He becomes even more alien to us because of the way in which he expresses his certainty, above all when he is talking about his own vocation and calling. God is now, according to him, hard at work on the final phase of his saving work which was begun in Christ. Paul has a decisive role to play here, by incorporating the Gentiles into the new people of God. Sometimes he talks about 'we apostles', and brings in the fellow Christians who share in his work. But everyone else is doing it wrong. Paul must have irritated many other Christians a great deal. We saw how agitated he got when 'apostles' invaded what he thought of as his own territory, the community in Corinth. From his point of view, we can understand why. But there were other ways of dealing with the Torah than Paul's. I am thinking now of the Christian communities in which the Gospel of Matthew was written. Jesus did not come to abolish the Law, but to fulfil it. Matthew's is the gospel in which Simon, who became Peter, was said to be the rock, the foundation of the new community. At the same time it is clear that Matthew's community was very much open to Christians from the Gentile world. Things could have been like this elsewhere. Nevertheless, authorities on the history of early Christianity still claim that Paul was indispensable; without him and his mission to the Gentiles, Christianity would have remained a sect within Judaism.

Paul was one of the leading figures in the variegated world of the first Christian generation. He was exceptional for his many-sided gifts, a mystic and an organizer, a theorist and a practical man, not to say a pragmatist, interested in how things would develop. He could be a Jew among Jews, a Gentile among Gentiles. But whatever he was had its foundation in the one great love which filled his life: the God who had drawn Paul to himself in Christ. So it is good for us to listen to Paul precisely because his strangeness provokes us into a constant pre-occupation with the central mystery of our life, and never allows us to leave it on one side.

TRANSLATOR'S NOTE

Fr Grollenberg has rightly been reluctant to clutter up the main text by giving precise sources of any quotations and, like him, I have used a variety of translations in quoting from Paul. English readers, however, may like to have references and details of English versions, and to know where other quotations come from. In the list below, the figures on the left refer to pages in this book.

16   The translation of the papyrus comes from C. K. Barrett (ed.), *The New Testament Background: Selected Documents*, SPCK 1956

42   Galatians 1.13–2.2 (New English Bible = NEB)

43   II Corinthians 11.32f. (Good News Bible = GNB)

45   Acts 15.6–11 (NEB)

46   Acts 15.20f. (GNB)

47   Galatians 2.2–5 (GNB); 2.9f. (NEB); Acts 15.28f. (GNB)

48   Galatians 2.14 (NEB)

51   The quotation is from an article by Rabbi Dow Marmur, 'A Jew Looks at the Christian Church', *Expository Times* LXXXVIII 8, May 1977, p. 238, who in turn is quoting Eugene Borowitz

59f.   I Thessalonians 4.15–17 (Revised Standard Version = RSV)

77f.   Galatians 4.13f., 15. Here and on pp. 94f., 111, I have made my own translation from the original Greek following Fr Grollenberg's rendering, to preserve the point he makes

79   Krister Stendahl, *Paul among Jews and Gentiles*, Fortress Press, Philadelphia and SCM Press 1977, p. 42

| 168 | Romans 12.18f.; 13.5f. (NEB) |
| 169 | Romans 15.30–32 (NEB) |

I would like to thank Fr Grollenberg for his care in checking over the manuscript and answering queries. Margaret Lydamore has left her mark on both the style and the content of the English version, Priscilla Hobson and Sarah Hillard typed out a near indecipherable manuscript, and the three between them gave the book its first (alas unpublished) English review.

JSB